DATE DUE
MAY 0 7 2003
WITHDRAWN

Mark
OF THE
Beast

Mark OF THE Beast

Death and Degradation in the Literature of the Great War

ALFREDO BONADEO

THE UNIVERSITY PRESS OF KENTUCKY

Scholarly publisher for the Commonwealth,
serving Bellarmine College, Berea College, Centre
College of Kentucky, Eastern Kentucky University,
The Filson Club, Georgetown College, Kentucky
Historical Society, Kentucky State University,
Morehead State University, Murray State University,
Northern Kentucky University, Transylvania University,
University of Kentucky, University of Louisville,
and Western Kentucky University.

Editorial and Sales Offices: Lexington, Kentucky 40506-0336

Library of Congress Cataloging-in-Publication Data

Bonadeo, Alfredo.
Mark of the beast : death and degradation in the literature of the Great War / Alfredo Bonadeo.
p. cm.
Includes index.
ISBN 0-8131-1680-5
1. European literature—20th century—History and criticism.
2. Italian literature—20th century—History and criticism.
3. World War, 1914-1918—Literature and the war. 4. World War, 1914-1918—Psychological aspects. 5. World War. 1914-1918—Moral and ethical aspects. 6. Death in literature. 7. War in literature.
I. Title. II. Title: Death and degradation in the literature of the Great War.
PN771.B66 1989
809'93354—dc19 88-27645

This book is printed on acid-free paper meeting
the requirements of the American National Standard
for Permanence of Paper for Printed Library Materials. ∞

Contents

Preface vii
1 The Animal Within 1
2 A Bath of Black Blood 50
3 A Loss beyond Life 95
Conclusion 150
Notes 152
Index 169

Preface

Many wars have been fought in modern times, but never before World War I did so many nations meet on the battlefield, never before were the resources of the combatants so fully engaged, and never before was human life destroyed on such a vast scale. One reason for the unprecedented destructiveness of the First World War was the new weaponry: the machine gun and the rapid-firing cannon, which brought about the "mechanization of killing." No effective defenses were devised against these lethal weapons, and battles were won and lost not by opposing steel to steel, but by hurling human flesh against metal. The tactic exacted a high price—and not only in bodies. Life in the trenches, exposure to death, and the prospect of mass slaughter made man desperate but tough, indifferent to loss of life but fearless, cruel but bold. The front took away from man his human self. He then found the will and the strength to fight and to face extermination, and he became instead a soldier.

Degradation infected the Great War. In some countries intellectuals and politicians thought, or imagined, that the common people had fallen low, and that the punishment of war and bloodshed would redeem them. Life was cheapened, and an obsession with bloodshed and death outweighed considerations of survival and victory. The political failure of the Risorgimento and the moral decay of the Italian people played a key role in Italy's intervention. On the eve of the conflict intellectuals and politicians detailed the nation's failings, exaggerated them, invented them if they did not exist, turned them into national guilt, and pointed to bloodshed and death as the means to wipe out what they viewed as the Italian shame.

Living with death led to despair, resignation, and suicidal impulses in the soldiers; some of them found death alluring. But death also brought out in a few exceptional men the spiritual strength that defied war and death itself.

This study, based on literary and historical sources, explains why men had to march to the front and shows how the front shaped their outlook on life and death. It may also show, despite a recent author's attempt to prove the opposite, that heroism in war "is obsolete,"[1] and that given a better understanding of what the battlefield does to man, battle may have "already abolished itself."[2]

Harry Steinhauer, Harry Lawton, Rhona Abel, Alex De Conde, Amanda Frost, and my wife, Barbara, have generously helped in drafting the manuscript, and I thank them all.

I also thank *Comparative Literature Studies* for permission to reprint "War and Degradation: Gleanings from the Literature of the Great War," which appears here in expanded form as the first chapter; and the Committee on Research at the University of California at Santa Barbara for supporting the project financially.

The translations are mine, unless otherwise indicated.

1. The Animal Within

War has often required the performance of extraordinary deeds and has often exacted incredible sacrifices from the combatant, but the European war of 1914-18 demanded more than previous conflicts. Six hundred thousand Italian soldiers were killed, and about one million were wounded; France lost almost one and a half million men, and its wounded totaled four million. Germany fared worse than France: almost two million killed and four million wounded. Yet, no matter how impressive, these statistics do not convey the drama of the men who returned outwardly unharmed after years of assaults and shellings during what Lewis Mumford has styled the "most deadly and vicious of all" wars, during the war in which armies were "reduced to the position of human cattle" and in which "the routine of the slaughterhouse" prevailed.[1]

Writing in 1930 of man's ability to exceed himself in combat, Douglas Jerrold tried to belittle the stress on men under fire in World War I. He argued that under ordinary circumstances man's endurance is limited; an engineer cannot operate an express train for twenty-four hours without a rest, nor can a surgeon operate for forty-eight hours without interruption. But under demanding conditions, such as those of the battlefield, where man must exert himself against great odds to survive, his ability for unusual effort increases considerably; men in the Great War, Jerrold concluded, found the resources needed to endure and to prevail over the danger, discomfort, and boredom of the front.[2] No doubt, the instinct of self-preservation pushed many combatants to acts that would be beyond an ordinary human being. But could soldiers punished by trench life muster such extraordinary strength without paying a price? Was there no moral or psychic cost to pay for the desperate struggle to survive? On the battlefields of World War I the prerequisite for bravery, for performing so-called superhuman tasks, was "the utilization of the whole reserve of moral force that lay in a man";[3] and this utilization wasted a man's inner resources. The waste changed man into an inferior being, and the price he paid for valor and survival was degradation.

Lord Julian Grenfell, the English captain who delighted in fighting in Flanders ("I adore war," he wrote to his mother in the fall of 1914), attributed his enjoyment neither to patriotism nor to courage, but to physical strength and to the instinct of the barbarian: "I have never felt so well, or so happy or enjoyed anything so much. It just suits my stolid health, and stolid nerves, and barbaric disposition."[4] Other combatants were not as comfortable with barbarity as Captain Grenfell. "It is a sweet and honourable thing" to die for one's country, an officer of the Royal Warwickshire Regiment wrote in Horatian vein from France in 1916. But he confessed that it was bitter "to have experienced the blood lust, to have killed for one's country and gloried in it," that it was "horrible" to come under "the primitive passion for slaughter . . . and to know that one was more than at liberty to give it full rein."[5] After fighting in the desert against the Turks, T.E. Lawrence recognized in *Seven Pillars of Wisdom* that battles "tore apart flesh and spirit."[6]

Was it guilt, remorse, or self-pity that prompted these reflections? Whatever the cause, they show that something went wrong with these men, even though victory and glory were theirs. The toll taken by the conflict, G.A. Panichas writes, was not just the physical death of millions of men; it was the "death of men in flesh and spirit."[7] War left many men physically alive but spiritually dead. One of the legacies of the war was the "lost generation," the soldiers unable to return to normal life because the war had turned them into misfits, into a "generation of men who, even though they may have escaped the shells, were destroyed by the war."[8] The legendary T.E. Lawrence, who, after the war and at the peak of life and fame, chose anonymity and expiation in the ranks of the Royal Air Force and Tank Corps, best represents that generation.

What happened inside the man who faced battle? During an attack "a man is no longer a man," realized the German student Gotthold von Rohden after a battle he remembered as "incomprehensible, inexplicable, irrational" in its bloodiness and destructiveness.[9] Two months of life at the front showed the Italian patriot Giani Stuparich that "the soul" was gone. "I look at my surviving comrades' faces," he wrote in the fall of 1915, "and I see in them the reflection of myself: it is painful to realize that in everyone's eyes the light of the soul is extinguished."[10] The Futurist artist Ardengo Soffici, an interventionist who fought as an officer on the Italian front, confessed that in battle the soul of the combatant "died," that he "shed his humanity" as he adapted himself to the "terrible and absurd" things that happened around him.[11] "To be a man" in the midst of battle, to keep one's human qualities in a world that denies humanity, wrote the French veteran Gabriel Chevallier, "is the ultimate horror."[12] Emilio Gadda, an officer of the Alpine Corps, caught with poetic flair the incompatibility of human life and life at the front. At the front, he wrote, "to be meant to disappear: to survive meant not to be." Even the "strong and brave" soldiers that Gadda met "shed their humanity to be soldiers of Italy."[13]

Father Agostino Gemelli, a chaplain on the Italian front, had keen insight into the source of soldierly boldness. He was at first unable to understand why the Italian soldiers, many of them uncultured and ignorant of the cause they were fighting for, took great risks during an action and often performed heroic feats. He soon realized that they fought well because a change had occurred in them; they "lost their individual personality" and "ceased to be men" for the duration of the action. When it was over and they returned to their line, they broke into tears or collapsed, signaling that another change had taken place: "Human nature took over again." They regained the human self that they had lost when they went into battle, and "became men again."[14]

Gemelli's sharp eye caught another aspect of the soldier's alienation from humanity: an estrangement from the "world," which was also alluded to by other Italian soldiers of the time and which figures prominently in recent literature dealing with the American soldier in Vietnam. Gemelli saw that in gradually detaching himself from "his own life," the soldier came to perceive the world as being split into "that of the trenches and the world far away from his own, the world of the civilians, of the rear, of the zone of peace." An officer told Gemelli that at the front he lived as if "a big screen had been erected between himself and the 'world,' as if he were looking on the affairs of the 'world' while leaning out of a window."[15] For the soldier at the front, the "world" held a special value and, like a condemned soul in Dante's Hell eager to hear about the "world" from a new arrival, he longed for any word of it to give him something he was constantly deprived of—comfort and pleasure. "The news of the other world, of that beautiful world that appeared to us like an Eden, far, far away in time and space, a world we had left without any hope of seeing it again," brought a new sense of life to Angelo Campodonico, a lieutenant fighting in the trenches of Mount Sei Busi.[16]

Adolfo Omodeo expressed the anguish that the soldier suffered from living in two irreconcilable worlds. He wrote to his wife in April 1916 from the battlefield: "Oh, were the toil of war only the march, the cold, the hunger, the trench; and were military virtue only the scorn of death! The true toil of war is holding up against the wear of each day lived in a different life . . . that seems to last forever and to interdict forever . . . the life already lived, the joy of fatherhood and of the family, the quiet work, the serene joys of the mind."[17] And for Carlo Salsa the separation from the world meant death. In a depressed moment on the slopes of Mount San Michele, he wrote: "Life seems reduced to this alone: our oblivion of the world, of a world that has forgotten us, to this wait for death."[18]

Sometimes the loss or shrinkage of the human self that allowed the soldier to excel on the battlefield was perceived as an advantage, as in the case of Filippo Rubè, the protagonist of Giuseppe Antonio Borgese's novel *Rubè,* who enlisted and was sent to the front as an officer. A southern Italian lawyer lacking an aim in life, who had a streak of cowardice, he sought war to redeem himself. The first time he came under fire, he smelled the "animal odor that his body breathed." He realized that "his spirit was devastated and almost empty," that it held nothing but "courage and fear," a mixture of feelings that wiped out all emotion: "Love and hatred were uprooted like little plants burnt out by a burst of fire. He looked for traces of love for the fatherland, but in vain." Nevertheless, changed into something between an automaton and an animal, Rubè marched on, "propelled forward by the spurts of an internal spring, lucid and precise, while a perfidious and delightful sensation pervaded his veins and set his nostrils quivering."[19]

The change that occurs in Rubè saves him from his reluctance to fight and from his fear. Similarly, Giovanni De Vita, one of the fallen officers whose letters were collected in a celebrated book by the historian Adolfo Omodeo, *Momenti della vita di guerra* (Moments in wartime life), wrote that in the trenches the combatant became indifferent, cynical, and "a beast." But De Vita saw a virtue in these qualities: if officers and soldiers alike did not become beasts, "there would be many suicides and only a few heroic acts" at the front.[20] Carlo Stuparich, the Italian patriot and combatant, described a relationship between bestiality and heroism, writing home with admiration for the degradation of the Italian soldiers: "These men are so heroic that they accept to be . . . more beastly than beasts."[21]

A man with his faculties intact would be unable to face the battlefield; he might even refuse to fight. Ernest Hemingway suggested that the soldier in combat suppress his imagination, warning that "a lack of ability to suspend the function of the imagination" would make the soldier unable to debase his own humanity, thereby turning him into a coward.[22] For Captain Liddell Hart, both a protagonist and a student of World War I, the deadening of the mind held the key to endurance and survival. He noted that to bear life and war on the Western Front, the soldier had to abolish the function of his intelligence, the faculty that distinguishes man from the beast: "The way to endurance lay primarily in deadening reflection with action" or with trivialities.[23] Paul Baumer, the protagonist of *All Quiet on the Western Front*, learns that survival requires exceptional daring and strength; to stay alive, he fights with more than human daring and strength, fights like an animal: "We [Baumer and his comrades] turn into animals when we go up to the line, because that is the only thing which brings us through safely." Inhabited by beings like Baumer, the line becomes the home of the beast: "The front is a cage."[24]

Lieutenant Montanelli is incredulous when he pays a visit to Emilio Lussu, an infantry officer on the Italian front and the author of *Un anno sull'altipiano* (One year on the upland), and finds Lussu in his dugout absorbed in the reading of *Orlando Furioso*. Montanelli asks: "Are you reading? . . . Are you not ashamed of yourself?" In his view, the life of the spirit at the front is dead. All the combatant wants is "to live, to live, to live . . . to drink and to live. Cognac. To sleep, to live, and cognac . . . and to think about nothing, because if we were to think we would kill one another." While Montanelli lectures on the advantages of deadening one's intelligence and soul, he unbuttons his raincoat and is seen to be naked from his shoulders to his knees: "Now I feel more like a man," he tells Lussu, "because I am more like an animal."[25] The state of the beast best fits the warrior.

Degradation changed the feeling and thought of the soldier about World War I, about his role in it, and about life's purpose; it was not a transitory and forgettable crisis as Liddell Hart and Hemingway seemed to imply. Robert Graves was one of those permanently altered. Two days after England declared war on Germany, he enlisted in the Royal Welch Fusiliers, a regiment with a glorious tradition, to avoid going to Oxford in October, and also "for the sake of war." He disdained the home duty of guarding prisoners, preferring to play a more heroic part in the war. He acted "soldierlike" and made himself "valuable" so that he might be chosen for front-line duty. When he was sent to France as a nineteen-year-old officer, he chose to go on patrol at the front as often as possible; having found out that the only thing respected in young officers was personal courage, he wanted to prove that he had it. He succeeded: regarded as having "more guts" than other junior officers, he was made a captain at the age of twenty.[26] Graves at this point had no misgivings about war and no reluctance in risking his life; he was, as one critic says, committed to "the values of courage and military efficiency."[27]

But he discovered that there was a limit to his courage because bravery before long destroys the brave. When the ill-fated offensive at Loos started in September 1915, Graves was standing on the fire step of the trench, aware that English troops were being decimated by their own misdirected machine-gun and artillery fire. As he prepared to go over the top and to lead his men to certain extermination, his mouth went dry, his eyes would not focus, and his legs began quaking under him. At that moment, he writes in his autobiography, "I found a waterbottle full of rum and drank about a half a pint; it quieted me down, and my head remained clear." Fortunately the attack was canceled, and the fighting poet was sent to the rear for a rest. But the self-confidence he had before Loos had left him forever. On his return to the trenches late in the fall "a black depression" and an apathy gripped him; he found "no excitement in patrolling, no horror in the continual experience of death."[28]

The use of alcohol, the depression, and the sudden loss of interest in heroism mark a turning point in Graves's story. The officer's collapse raises a question: why and how did soldiers continue to fight when the mainspring of action wound down? An officer, Graves explains, was nearly useless for the first three weeks in the trenches because he lacked experience. After adjustment his performance improved, and he reached a peak within a few months unless he was wounded or killed. If he escaped injury, decline then set in and "neurasthenia developed. At six months he was still more or less all right; but by nine or ten months. . . . he usually became a drag on the other company officers. After a year . . . he was often worse than useless." The reason for an officer's stamina during the first few months at the front was physiological—the "stimulating chemical" pumped into his blood by his own body kept the officer on the go. But after nine months or so the endocrine organ, presumably strained and disabled, stopped secreting the tonic fluid into the bloodstream. At that point an officer became apathetic, and his endurance decreased dramatically. Since headquarters did not take into account such deterioration, officers were kept at the line as long as needed, rather than being shifted when they could no longer take it. How did they manage to lead and to fight when they were no longer fit for duty? Drink was their answer; they became "dipsomaniacs."[29]

"O God," Cassio exclaims in disbelief in *Othello* after drunkenness has led him to a disorderly fight, "that men should put an enemy in their mouths to steal away their brains! That we should, with joy, pleasance, revel and applause, transform ourselves into beasts!"[30] Cassio felt a beast because he drank and then brawled. At the front, many British officers drank heavily and, like Cassio in *Othello*, lost their heads and acted like beasts. Graves knew officers who "had worked up to the point of two bottles of whiskey a day." One of them, a company commander, sent virtually all of his men to their death in three successive actions because, the poet understates, he was no longer capable of "making clear decisions."[31]

Graves continued to fight until he was wounded, even winning a citation from his colonel for disregard of death. But war left deep scars on his life. He became neurasthenic and, back in England, fear of gas obsessed him, sharp noises sent him diving to the ground, and "nightmares of bursting shells and waking hallucinations" tormented him for several years. In *Good-bye to All That*, he writes that it took him ten years for his "blood to recover."[32] Even so, Graves says tersely in one verse of *Recalling War*, the spiritual loss was as great as the physical one: "Our youth became all-flesh and waived the mind."[33]

The degradation of reasoning powers by means of alcohol was not confined to British officers. Because alcohol "induces the appearance and feeling of courage,"[34] drink was frequently used as the means to what Liddell Hart and Hemingway regarded as the end sought by the soldier at the front—the suppression of reflection and imagination, the reduction of man to an unthinking, fearless being for the sake of fighting efficiency. The use of alcohol was widespread among Italian troops, for instance. It rid them of the understanding of what they were in for, and it gave them the strength to attack the enemy when chances of survival were slim. For the Italian headquarters, alcohol produced such good results that its use at the front became "institutionalized."[35] Cognac was liberally dispensed before throwing the troops into suicidal actions, and the soldiers who recognized its function—that of making them do what reason told them not to do—called it their "gasoline."[36] But they were also aware that cognac changed them into beasts to be sent to their death. When in Lussu's *Un anno sull'altipiano* a company paymaster orders five men to the rear to fetch chocolate and cognac, the troops know that a hopeless attack is imminent, that they are animals marked for slaughter. One of the soldiers exclaims: "They fatten the pig really well before killing him"; others respond: "They fatten it well. They fatten us well."[37]

Captain Lussu's experience allows the narrator of *Un anno sull'altipiano* to impart to the use of alcohol at the front a wider and perhaps more interesting meaning than Grave's book does. Through the words and behavior of Colonel Abbati, a battalion commander whom Lussu meets three times in the course of the narrative, the author of *Un anno* hints at degradation by alcohol as the basis of war making. A career officer against his will, the colonel sees the war and the tactics of battle as an absurdity that he has to defend himself and his honesty against by means of alcohol. The colonel, his mind already cracking under the stress of war and alcohol when Lussu meets him the first time, believes that every soldier must drink to endure war, and in discovering that Lussu abstains from liquor, he is compelled to record in his diary what he views as a rare exception: "Met abstemious lieutenant. June 5, 1916." Colonel Abbati's prize possession in the field is *The Art of Making Liquors by Oneself,* a book whose contents the colonel must have mastered, for every time he appears he is carrying a bottle and a glass and he takes a drink. This war, he tells Lussu, "is not a war of infantrymen against infantrymen, of artilleries against artilleries. It is a war of wine cellars against wine cellars, of casks against casks, of bottles against bottles." A humanist (at the top of his college class in Italian literature before the family forced him into military school), Colonel Abbati laments the impersonal and mechanical ways of modern war, which feed his thirst for liquor. "I have been fighting on all sides of the front for more than one year now," he points out to Lussu in the summer of 1916, "but I have never seen the face of an Austrian soldier. Yet we kill one another daily. Killing one another without knowing one another, without seeing one another! It's horrible! This is why we all get drunk, on both sides."[38]

Almost as if to confirm Colonel Abbati's words in chapter 5 on the inevitability of alcohol at the front, chapter 6 gives Lussu's impression of an attack by drunken Austrian infantrymen: "The wind was blowing toward us. From the Austrian side was blowing a heavy, dense odor of cognac, as if it were released from damp wine cellars kept shut for many years. As the Austrians sang and shouted hurrah! it seemed that the doors were thrown open and that the wine cellars flooded us with cognac. That cognac reached my nostrils in waves, seeped into my lungs, and stuck there with the stench of tar, gasoline, resin, and sour wine mixed together." Despite the stimulus of the cognac, the Austrians are repulsed by the Italian counterattack with bayonets, but Lussu is unable to recall what happened during the counterattack because, he writes, "the stench of that cognac had left me stunned."[39]

When Captain Lussu meets Colonel Abbati for the last time at the end of *Un anno sull'altipiano*, the colonel has changed so much that Lussu can hardly recognize him. Abbati asks Lussu if he, too, has begun to drink, although adding that he is no longer sure about the need for alcohol. "The question,"he says "is more complex than I had thought before." The reason the colonel is no longer sure that alcohol is beneficial is that drink has brought him to his end. "I am," he says, "a finished man." Lussu sees him as "haggard, old . . . his eyes sunk in . . . tired, and sick." "Colonel Abbati," the colonel himself proclaims, "has managed to kill the sense of war, but cognac has killed Colonel Abbati." While alcohol has solved some of his problems at the front, it has nevertheless killed his mind. Degradation enabled him to perform his military duties, at least up to mid-1917, but it also killed his mind; Colonel Abbati is about to go mad.[40]

Under fire, when combat left no time for the philosophical reflections and leisurely drinking, alcohol was sometimes brutally craved as the means to kill "the sense of war." To silence Austrian machine guns during a night attack near Mount Zebio that pinned down whatever was left of his battalion, Lussu crawled away from no-man's-land to seek help. Reaching the Italian battalion stationed to the left of his own, he meant to ask the commander for support fire, but this battalion was now under fire, and confusion and fear reigned. The commander, a nameless major in Lussu's narrative, was standing near the command post leaning against a fir tree, his face red and very excited.

> "Hurry!" he shouted. But nobody showed up. While I was getting closer to him, the major continued: "Hurry! Hurry or I'll kill you! Give me the cognac! the cognac!" He didn't shout. He screamed in a very high-pitched voice, with the tone of a drill instructor, as if he were addressing not a person, but a unit, a battalion on the parade ground. He said 'cognac' with the same tone of voice as if, from the saddle, he had ordered 'Battalion ready' or 'Form double column.' Finally, as I got close to him, a panting soldier showed up. He held a bottle of cognac in his hand. His arm extended, he held the bottle high, as if it were a flag. . . . The major clutched a gun in his right hand and a piece of paper in his left.

> He threw the paper down and advanced to meet the soldier, still screaming: "Give it to me! Give it to me!" He brandished the bottle and, with lightning-like motion, he glued it to his mouth. His head thrown back, immobile, he seemed petrified. He looked like a dead man standing on its feet. Only the throat, which gulped the liquor with jerks that sounded like wailings, gave signs of life.

Lussu speaks to the major when he has finished, but the drunken officer only smiles and remains silent. He is now unable to give orders; subordinate officers are trying to do what is his duty.[41] Yet if one ignores what Lussu knew, the major at his command post, unflinching under fire, might be said to defy danger and death.

Degradation needed no alcohol to find its way into the bones of the soldier. Siegfried Sassoon volunteered for service three days before England entered the war, was commissioned, like Graves, in the Royal Welch Fusiliers, and was posted to France, where he shared military experiences with the author of *Good-bye to All That*. As an infantry officer Sassoon fought valiantly on the Somme and was decorated, his daring exploits earning him the nickname of "Mad Jack." As he writes in the *Memoirs of an Infantry Officer*, the record of his wartime years, Sassoon wanted "the War to be an impressive experience, terrible, but not horrible enough" to interfere with his heroic emotions.[42] He wanted to be able to look on his war deeds as a clean, noble experience. He was bound to be disappointed.

Just before marching from the rear to the front line to take part in the battle of Arras, Sassoon sits on a tree stump in the park of a chateau. It is a peaceful evening in the spring of 1917, and Sassoon feels confident, serene, and even excited at the prospect of imminent battle. This emotion is not new to him, but for the first time in the war he questions it. Why, he asks himself, should I feel enthusiasm about facing the enemy and death? He becomes suspicious of his own sincerity, and then realizes his emotion is as phony as that expressed by junior officers going to the front: "Never has life brought me such an abundance of noble feelings."[43] What prompted Sassoon to question his emotions and discover his insincerity?

The war, Sassoon realizes that evening in the park of the chateau, has been more terrible than he had expected, and despite his resolve to keep its horror from spoiling a heroic experience, war has sapped his strength. He was probably reaching the point, identified by Graves in *Good-bye to All That*, where an officer is simply worn out and starts to break down. But Sassoon's crisis is far from physiological, and he needs something other than alcohol to restore his endurance, real or illusory. His crisis calls for moral strength, not for physical remedies. But inside Sassoon there remains only a patriotic spirit, which has no power to support him as he faces the loss of the "humanities" that give meaning to his life at the front. At this point in the war all he believes in is the "battalion spirit"—sharing his life with the other officers and the troops, and gaining their respect and affection.

The battalion spirit is all the "humanity" left in him. But war has taught him the "impermanence of its humanities." On one evening he might be with comrades in a cozy room in London, enjoying music and conversation, and within a week "a single machine gun or a few shells might wipe out the whole picture." He remembers with anguish the battalion that was "part of his life" the previous year; by September the battalion had lost almost all its men, and Sassoon had narrowly escaped with his life. Now, just before the battle of Arras, he feels the threat of the same kind of loss he incurred a year earlier, but he has no strength to face it. "That was the bleak truth," he confesses, "and there was only one method of evading it; to make a little drama out of my own experience—that was the way out. I must play at being a hero in shining armor, as I'd done last year; if I didn't, I might crumple up altogether." Faced with the loss of the "humanities" that made sense of his life at the front, Sassoon lets the waves of patriotic rhetoric rise in him and save him from collapse. He decides on "death and glory," and forgetful of the insincerity of his emotion, gets up from the tree stump with a sense of having solved his problems.[44]

But they are not solved. The emotion that rouses Sassoon to be hero in shining armor, boosting his morale on the eve of the battle, fails him when a little later he enters the front line, "that zone of inuhuman havoc," to meet the "gloom and disaster of the thing called Armageddon. . . a dreadful place, a place of horror and desolation which no imagination could have invented." As he sloshes through the mud, Sassoon sees immobile soldiers huddled against the walls of the trenches; the ghastly light of the flares grotesquely distorts their appearance, and to Sassoon's sinking spirit and mind they look like corpses standing erect. At this moment he realizes that only an animal can endure in this place: "And I saw it then, as I see it now. . . a place where a man of strong spirit might know himself utterly powerless against death and destruction, and yet stand up and defy gross darkness and stupefying shell-fire, discovering in himself the invincible resistance of an animal or an insect, and an endurance which he might, in after days, forget or disbelieve."[45] Having found the strength of the animal, Sassoon is again taken by the rhetoric of heroism, and during the action that follows he forgets the world of Armageddon. Not even a wound in the shoulder can stop him now; he begins to feel rabidly heroical, "ready for any suicidal exploit." He prepares to launch himself and his seventy-five men into a "rash and irrelevant" attack, but the project luckily fizzles when the relief company comes up the line.[46]

The experience on the battlefield of Arras turned Sassoon

against war. While convalescing in England during the summer of 1917 he wrote a letter of condemnation, which a group of pacifists led by Bertrand Russell managed to have read in the House of Commons. The letter was risky business for Sassoon. His friend Robert Graves convinced the military authority that his fellow officer, shell-shocked, could not be held reponsible for his words, sparing him the court martial. Sassoon was confined to Craiglockhart War Hospital, but he, like Graves, later returned to the front, where he was again wounded.

Both Sassoon and Graves went back to the front to share and relieve the suffering of the men in the trenches. Sassoon could no longer enjoy the safety and warmth of his home; the thought of men "strangely isolated from ordinary comforts in the dark desolation of murderously-disputed trench sectors" tormented his conscience, and he, like Graves, wanted "to make things easier" for the men under his command.[47] Sassoon went back to the front to fight "the foul beast of war that bludgeons life,"[48] not to fight for victory.

Life at the front tested not only the soldier who repudiated war after seeing its face, but also the soldier who accepted war as a neccessity and who professed imperviousness to its horrors. In *The Middle Parts of Fortune* (better known before 1977 as *Her Private We*), Frederic Manning represents graphically the brutality and waste of the battlefield (the book reminded Hemingway of "how things really were" in war),[49] but he accepts war "as a total and inescapable experience and does not speculate about the possibility of things being otherwise."[50] The bravery that Manning, who served on the Somme as a private in the King's Shropshire Light Infantry, injects into his novels' characters has nothing of the patriotic rhetoric that helped Sassoon to play the hero. Manning stresses the value of strength in the face of death and suffering, the role of determination ("to stick to it"), and the worth of heroism as a struggle to "overcome . . . fear."[51] The moral of his book: "One must not break."[52] Though he rises above the burden of war, Manning nevertheless will sink below his humanity.

Toward the end of the novel Manning contrasts the "enthusiasm" that brought him and his comrades into the army with the "long and bitter agony they endured afterwards." They had gone to war to prove themselves better than their natures were: "It was the unknown which they had challenged; and when the searching flames took hold of their very flesh, the test was whether or not they should flinch under them. The men knew it. We can stick to it, they said; and they had . . . to master their pitiful human weaknesses."[53] By what means and how successfully did they overcome their human weaknesses?

When Private Bourne, the protagonist of the novel, comes back from the first bloody action exhausted and collapses in the dugout, he is "indifferent to everything." Standing before this image of dejection an officer predicts that pain and fear will never leave the men at the front: "If our luck holds we'll keep moving out of one bloody misery into another." During the night Bourne hears "convulsive agonies" from his sleeping comrades in the darkness: "Lips parted with the sound of a bubble bursting, teeth met grinding as the jaws worked, there were little whimperings which quickened into sobs, passed into long shuddering moans, or culminated in angry, half-articulated obscenties, and then relapsed, with fretful, uneasy movements and heavy breathing, into a more profound sleep. . . . The darkness seems to him to be filled with the shudderings of tormented flesh."

Unable to sleep, Bourne sits up, lights a cigarette, and relives the phases of the day's action, still alive in the agonized unconscious of his sleeping comrades: the tension of waiting before going over the top, the effort to move toward the enemy, the dread that filled him, the paralyzing feeling that "one cannot hurry, alone, into nowhere, into nothing." He recalls the terrifying explosions, the "men smashed . . . rent and strewn in bloody fragments," and the "infinitely . . . horrible and revolting" sight of a "man shattered and eviscerated."[54]

If such recollections alone can throw soldiers into "convulsive agonies," then living through the real thing might very well break them. But neither Bourne nor his comrades seem to break. They have gained an extrordinary endurance, which Manning calls despair, instinct's power ("Heroism . . . is indistinguishable from despair"), something that keeps them from crumpling. During the attack that haunted Bourne's memory in the night, "something had changed" inside the protagonist, Manning recalls. When the heat of the action had generated in Bourne the "instinct of the beast," he then attacked without thought and without fear: "The conflict and tumult of his mind had gone, to have contracted and hardened within him; fear remained . . . but that too, seemed to have been beaten and forged into a point of exquisite sensibility. . . . Only the instinct of the beast survived in him, every sense was alert and in that tension was some poignancy."

Unlike the soldiers that Father Gemelli had observed on the Italian front, Bourne and his comrades stayed in the grip of the beast after a battle. The routine of the following morning (they "tightened their belts, hawked, and spat in the dust") reveals something vulgar and insolent about them. They want "to lie hidden" until they have "regained control of themselves," until their behavior becomes less beastly; like members of a herd, they "instinctively" help each other in satisfying their physical needs. Finally the soldiers submit to the "inexorable routine" of the body, to the animal urge that sends them to an "unscreened trench which served as a latrine." This was furnished with a pole, and they sat on this insecure perch at either end of piled-up solids; while they sat, "they hunted and killed the lice on their bodies."

This record of the activities on the morning following a battle extends the image of the beast that took shape during the attack. "They had been through it," Manning comments, "and having been through, they had lapsed a little lower than savage, into the mere brute."[55]

Manning's soldiers remain prisoners of their new state of being. While at the rear of the lines for a rest, Bourne realizes he gets along well with his comrades and would like to know more about them, about what they did in civilian life. But he feels that there is no point in asking questions because what they were and what they did before the war means nothing now. War has changed them and reduced them all to a life that negates the humanity of their past. "Men had reverted to a more primitive stage in their development, and had become nocturnal beasts of prey, hunting each other in packs. . . . There is an extraordinary veracity in war, which strips man of every conventional covering he has, and leaves him to face a fact as naked and as inexorable as himself." And when Bourne realizes that he and his fellow soldiers Martlow and Shem have become friends, he cannot understand how a human bond such as friendship could grow among men who have lost their humanity: he "wondered what was the spiritual thing in them which lived and seemed to grow stronger in the midst of beastliness."[56]

The "instincts of the beast" that drove the soldiers against the enemy line at the beginning of the novel emerge again during the major, final combat. Just as extreme alertness of the senses displaced fear at the start of the earlier attack, the fear vanished when Bourne went over the top and rushed the German trenches: "He felt himself moving more freely, as though he had full control of himself." As he advanced, confident and unhurt, "a kind of maniacal rage filled him" and soon a "triumphant frenzy thrust him forward." Finally, his senses were subverted: "The effort and rage in him . . . made him pant and sob, but there was some strange intoxication of joy in it. . . . The extremities of pain and pleasure had met and coincided too."

The masochistic element, the transformation of pain into pleasure, represents a new twist in Bourne's degradation. The death of his buddy Martlow during the attack intensifies that degradation. The instinct of the beast takes physical shape: like a wolf about to sink its teeth into the prey, "teeth clenched and bared, the lips snarling back from them in exultation," Bourne redoubles his effort at killing the Germans.[57]

The fiction and reality of the Great War often blend the kind of exaltation and degradation that drive the protagonists of Manning's novel. Before the attack in which he will be wounded, the socioeconomist Richard H. Tawney, a sergeant on the Somme in the summer of 1916, worries about getting scared, losing his head, and causing his men to be needlessly killed. He makes an effort to control his fears and to convince himself that he is all right, that there is no danger. He then cautiously leads his men through no-man's-land. When he realizes that despite this self-control many of his men have been killed and he sees the Germans only a hundred yards in front of him, a new energy and drive take hold of him. "The sight of the Germans drove everything else out of my head," he writes; and as he starts shooting at them he makes a discovery: "Most men . . . have a Paleolithic savage somewhere in them, a beast that occasionally shouts to be given a chance of showing his joyful cunning in destruction." The beast, the powerful single-mindedness blinded by a sadistic pleasure in destruction, helps Tawney to destroy the enemy; his fire drops every German in sight except one whom Tawney repeatedly shoots at, but misses. Then he understands better the working of the beast: "I missed more than once. I was puzzled and angry. . . . It was missing I hated. That's the beastliest thing in war. One's like a merry, mischievous ape tearing up the image of God."[58]

After a few months at the front, the poet and literary critic

Herbert Read thinks that he can "endure the experience of war" even at its worst, and that the horror of war does not "necessarily mean a deadening of the sensiblity." He admits, however, that fear and loneliness open the mind "to the electric uprush of the animal." During the raid he led on the enemy's lines on a summer night in 1917, a raid which he describes as representative of his experience of war, he feels the uprush of the animal, and he welcomes it because he needs it. The uprush of the beast gives him inhuman strength, and carries him through the exchange of shots and the animal utterances. When he approaches the unseen enemy in the dark, he suddenly takes heart. "I was filled with a great exaltation," he writes, "my body did not exist, save as a wonderfully unconsious mechanism. I gave a great inhuman cry and dashed forward, barking with my Colt at the shadowy figures not ten yards away. One gave a wild bestial shriek and fell into the darkness. . . . I ran on, impelled by an unknown energy."[59] Familiar with the surge of the animal in men at the front, Read represented that singular experience in poetry. He lends to the soldier in battle hallucinatory wildness:

> His wild heart beats with painful sobs,
> His strained hands clench an ice-cold rifle,
> His aching jaws grip a hot parched tongue,
> And his wide eyes search unconsciously.
> He cannot shriek.
> Bloody saliva
> Dribbles down his shapeless jacket.
> I saw him stab
> and stab again
> A well-killed Boche.[60]

Graves, Sassoon, Manning, and their generation were the sons of a country whose glory and power had grown upon its military might, and its might upon generations of citizen-soldiers. Among the upper classes and the intellectuals, those who understood best the history of the English nation and its achievement, war, victory, and conquest bred pride, a sense of duty, and the will to make sacrifices. In his poem "1914" Rupert Brooke, the representative of the British heroic generation, thanked God for war: "Now God be thanked who has matched us with this hour"; and in the war he saw the revival of the national heritage:

> Honour has come back . . .
> And Nobleness walks in our ways again,
> And we have come into our heritage.

England, Brooke wrote, would be shamed if it did not go to war and if no Englishmen died in it.[61] The generation of 1914 revered England, and took up, at least at the beginning of the conflict, "the country's cause and accepted lightheartedly the likelihood of early death."[62] This generation knew of the "heroic values" that T.E. Hulme theorized about just before the outbreak of the war: objective, absolute, and independent of subjective feeling, and characterized by "irrationality,"[63] values that demanded heroism for heroism's sake. This generation felt that war was "the ultimate test of a nation's manhood, the ultimate proof of its vigor and of its right to exist." Brute force was manly.[64]

But was it? Just after the war broke out Bertrand Russell wrote that the feeling, then rife in both England and Europe, that war is the ultimate test of a nation's manhood comes from the belief that superiority in "physical force" is the most desirable form of primacy. The belief in this kind of superiority, he retorted, is a barbarous standard; the systems of justice of the civilized countries condemn and punish those citizens guilty of violence. On the international level, however, nations have been deaf to the voice of reason and justice. They still try to gain dominance one over the other by violence, and on the battlefields of Europe do daily "astonishing acts of ferocity." What happens there shows the savagery of nations and peoples—not their heroism and manhood. To endure at the front, men must adjust, and such accommodation destroys all humane feeling. In almost every man, the British philosopher explained, "there is a wild beast slumbering. . . but civilized men know that it must not be allowed to awake." Had civilized men stayed out of the war, they might have gone through life "without ever having the wild beast in them aroused." But in choosing to fight, they have now fallen under "the domain of the wild beast." The transformation of man into beast on the battlefield, Russell feared, is permanent and telling. The change subverts all of life, not just the time spent at the front. Those who fall under the domain of the wild beast lose moral self-respect, integrity, and uprightness, and the loss compromises their future. "A secret shame" makes soldiers possessed by the wild beast "cynical and despairing, without the courage that sees facts as they are, without the hope that makes them better. War is perpetrating this moral murder in the souls of vast millions of combatants; every day many are passing over to the dominion of the brute by acts which kill what is best within them."[65]

But resistance to the call of the "wild beast" was very difficult, especially for those who on the battlefield had found out that there was no choice between survival and degradation. Besides, words that disparaged peace and the humanitarian ideal , while extolling the beast in man, were spoken by men as authoritative as Russell. At about the same time that Russell indicted the "wild beast,"another distinguished philosopher, the Italian Benedetto Croce, glorified it. In March 1916 he attacked Socialism because it propounded an idea that he scorned: the "peaceful existence of the proletarians of all the countries" in the world. War in history, Croce argued, shows that international struggles matter more than social concerns and that peoples and states, not classes, make history. War has shaken and "almost destroyed the humanitarian ideology." Above all, war has shown that man has no sense of brotherhood, that in him lives "the bloodthirsty animal,"which is winning freedom of action during the war now in progress. Croce calls this animal the "hero ready to throw away his life and all kind of goods to defend a flag." When the humanitarians describe war as "a barbarous vestige, the survival of the bloodthirsty instinct," they show the incurable inferiority, the meanness, and the obtuseness of the humanitarian mind. Magnetized by the "bloodthirsty animal," Croce with murderous flair styled the European conflict a "religious holocaust."[66]

The wild beast mauled Graves, Sassoon, and Manning, but they recovered their human selves and after the war returned to normal life. Other victims, however, were unable to recover; they lost the "best within them" for good, showing that letting loose the "bloodthirsty animal" to "defend a flag" exacted a price that Croce had not foreseen in his theories.

When at twenty-eight T.E. Lawrence became the organizer and leader of the Arab Revolt, he had no personal or psychic problems; he was an odd sort of genius, but was not even especially introspective. Intelligence, political experience, and the qualities of the leader distinguished him. When he left the army in the summer of 1919 he was a national figure and could have obtained prestigious jobs in government or industry, but he neglected such opportunities. He first worked briefly with Winston Churchill on the political settlement of the Middle East, then plunged into the composition of *Seven Pillars of Wisdom*, the record of his years among the Arabs in revolt. In July 1922 he joined the Royal Air Force as Private Ross, but was expelled only a few months later. Not long after, in the spring of 1923, he enlisted in the Tank Corps, again in the ranks, under a new false name—Shaw. In 1925 he finally managed to get back into the Air Force, where he served until February 1935, three months before his death.

Why was it that Lawrence withdrew from the world and, as Herbert Read imaginatively put it, "immured himself in what he thought was the nearest modern equivalent of a monastery of the Middle Ages"—the military?[67] Why did he become an "Outsider" in a "tragedy of waste"?[68] Having lost belief in himself, his motive power sapped,[69] Lawrence had reached the point of being unable to take care of himself (one reason he joined the Royal Air Force). The war in the desert left him extremely introspective, "troubled by guilt and shame," and powerless to regain a sense of his own worth.[70] One of his friends, Eric Kennington, wrote that in the years after the war Lawrence struggled "to reclaim or re-create his soul."[71] If what Kennington wrote is true, war must have robbed the ex-guerrilla leader of something very valuable, which in peacetime he tried in vain to regain.

A recent biographical study, however, concludes that in the aftermath of the war, Lawrence was trying to debase himself, not to rise above degradation. Lawrence, the biographer writes, had "a powerful need for penance through degradation and humiliation, a need that was accompanied by a permanently lowered self-regard" and by the desire to be treated like a beast—a "compulsive wish to be whipped."[72]

Moral and physical masochism indeed troubled T.E. Lawrence after the war. "The army seems safe against enthusiasm. It's a horrible life . . . and . . . self-degradation is my aim," he writes to his friend Lionel Curtis from the Tank Corps in March 1923.[73] In the same letter he hints at his own bestiality: "The Army (which I despise with all my mind) is more natural than the R.A.F.," "natural" being a word that Lawrence "frequently used to denote the primitive or bestial aspect of life."[74] He returns to the theme of bestiality in another letter, to Edward Garnett, in April: "The Army is unspeakable: more solidly animal than I believed Englishmen could be." And later in the same letter: "It's an odd penance to have set oneself to live amongst animals for seven years. Nebuchadnezzar did it, I suppose. . . . Do you think Nebuchadnezzar made himself animal like his companions? I thought of trying to write about him."[75]

The reflection on Nebuchadnezzar throws more light on Lawrence's degradation than on the Babylonian king's. At the height of his power Nebuchadnezzar, a cruel military leader,was "banished from the society of men" and, in the words of the Bible, he lived "with the wild beasts." He ate "grass like oxen; his body was drenched by the dew of heaven, until his hair grew long like goats' hair and his nails like eagles' talons."[76] Lawrence, at the height of success and fame, banished himself from all society and demeaned himself by living among men whom he regarded as animals.

"These masses," Lawrence writes again to Curtis about his comrades, "are as animal, as carnal as were their ancestors before Plato and Christ and Shelley and Dostoevsky taught and thought." He tells Curtis how he submits to degradation: "You've got to take this black core of things in camps, this animality, on trust." Sometimes degradation weighs heavily on Lawrence ("these soldiers are foul-mouthed, and behind their mouths is a pervading animality of spirit, whose unmixed bestiality frightens me and hurts me"),[77] but he does nothing to escape from it.

Why did Lawrence choose to live in a state of perennial degradation after the war? What did the war in the desert do to him? The war degraded him, and when the killing stopped, he found it hard to be a human being again. Like Manning, Lawrence admired heroism and wanted to be heroic. While leading his Arab army to Akaba in May 1917, Lawrence tells in *Seven Pillars of Wisdom*, a strong, hot, dry wind blew across the desert; it shriveled and cracked lips, chapped faces, and ate into eyelids. The Arabs covered their heads and faces with brow-folds to protect their skin, but the leader intrepidly disdained shelter: "For my part," he writes "I always rather liked a *khamsin* [the wind], since its torment seemed to fight against mankind with ordered conscious malevolence, and it was pleasant to outface it so directly, challenging its strength, and conquering its extremity."[78] At times Lawrence reached "a cruel extreme of endurance," but he claims that never "was there an intimation of physical break." Only "moral weakness" could have broken him, but at this point of the narrative Lawrence held up.

Like Manning, the leader of the Arab Revolt shows bravery in the face of adversity; and like Manning, he discovers that heroism takes a heavy toll. His body holds up, but his soul goes to pieces. Battle, unlike nature, brings Lawrence's spirit down. To be sure, fighting represents a personal test and an occasion for the will to overcome "moral weakness"—fear. But battle also changes him, and although he is reluctant to say how ("into the sources of my energy of will I dared not to probe"), he implicitly admits that the power of the animal, the same force that drives the soldier on the European fronts, drives him, too, against the enemy in the desert: "While we rode we were disbodied, unconscious of flesh or feeling."[79]

Some critics suspect that, despite military success, Lawrence had no heroic temper. In his review of *Seven Pillars of Wisdom*, Herbert Read wrote that the book fails as epic because its protagonist is "not heroic," and that he is no hero because he questions himself, his aims, his destiny; he shows too much doubt about himself and about what he is doing.[80] A biographer, more explicit about the absence of heroism in Lawrence, notes that the guerrilla leader helped to make out of date the kind of heroism made of blind patriotism and glorification of war that Lawrence's generation idealized.[81] Heroism eluded *Seven Pillars of Wisdom* because Lawrence's personal loss—the destruction of his humanity recorded in his book along with his military successes—turned what could have been a "triumph," as the subtitle of *Seven Pillars of Wisdom* indicates, into a defeat.

Toward the conclusion of the Arab Revolt, Lawrence writes: "In my last five actions I had been hit, and my body so dreaded further pain that now I had to force myself under fire. Generally I had been hungry: lately always cold: and frost and dirt had poisoned my hurts into a festering mass of sores."[82] Here is a man who obeys duty, who endures, and who gives much of himself, but who is uninspired by his deeds. He is conscious of his suffering, but unconscious of the motive for his sacrifice; he knows he is reaching the end of his tether, but he ignores the driving force. He ignores it because the human cost of his exploits concerns him more than the military gains. When the unconsciousness of flesh and feeling—what Lawrence sees as the source of the combatant's aggressive power, of his "excitement"—faded, the soldiers, Lawrence writes in the context of the difficult winter campaign by the Dead Sea at the end of 1917, saw their bodies "with some hostility, with a contemptuous sense that they reached their highest purpose not as vehicles of the spirit, but when, dissolved, their elements served to manure a field."

This contempt for the body has one meaning for the Arabs, and another for Lawrence. The Arabs believed in the "antithesis between flesh and spirit," and when physically exhausted they preserved the independence of the spirit from the body and the wholeness of their soul. But Lawrence, with a "perverse sense of values," conceived of body and spirit as "one" entity, and, fortified in his "nihilist attitude" by the practice of the revolt, he let his whole being be dragged down to the level of his body, to vile matter, only good "to manure a field."[83]

The burden of organizing and leading the desert fighters complicated and reinforced Lawrence's degradation. His estrangement from humanity sets the tone of *Seven Pillars of Wisdom*, for it appears in the first chapter. "We were," Lawrence writes of himself and of his band of fighting Arabs, "a self-centered army without parade or gesture, devoted to freedom"; they were, it would seem, a well-organized unit with a noble goal. But the fight to free an oppressed people has no power to inspire Lawrence because he knows that he himself must submit to a slavery that destroys his soul: "We had sold ourselves into its [freedom's] slavery, manacled ourselves together in a chain-gang . . . and we had surrendered, not body alone, but soul to the overmastering greed of victory." As a result the rebels in the desert had become less than human—they "lost the world," they were "drained of morality, of volition, of responsibility like dead leaves in the wind." Even intimate contact reveals the disintegrating effect of the desert war on the warriors: "Gusts of cruelty, perversions, lusts ran lightly over the surface" without troubling the men. Sexuality degenerates into "hot flesh and blood" that "tormented their bellies with strange longings," and sodomy becomes a driving force of the revolt: "Some began to justify this sterile process, and swore that friends quivering together in the yielding sand with intimate hot limbs in supreme embrace, found there hidden in the darkness a sensual co-efficient" of the war effort.[84]

At this point in his story Lawrence shrinks back, as if he wants to dissociate himself from the cause and the race he fought for and to hold off the degradation that engulfs him. He protests that he "was sent to these Arabs as a stranger, unable to think their thoughts or subscribe to their beliefs." He cannot deny the role he plays among the Arabs, but he implicitly repudiates it by warning a hypothetical leader that warring among alien people means trading the soul for a beast, which he admits he has become: "Pray God that men reading the story will not . . . go out to prostitute themselves and their talents in serving another race. A man who gives himself to be a possession of aliens leads a Yahoo life, having bartered his soul to a brute-master." The sense of degradation, which makes Lawrence's role in the revolt "increasingly odious and disturbing to him personally," is the motif that brings the first chapter of *Seven Pillars of Wisdom* to conclusion. The image is that of a man who is losing his highest human attribute, reason: "His body plodded on mechanically, while his reasonable mind left him, and from without looked down critically on him . . . . Sometimes these selves would converse in the void; and then madness was very near."[85]

On the occasion of his thirtieth birthday (August 1918 in Bair), Lawrence assesses himself and finds no good reason for self-respect because he has given in to the beast, a surrender he likes and at the same time detests: "I liked the things underneath me and took my pleasures and adventures downward. There seemed a certainty in degradation, a final safety. Man could rise to any height, but there was an animal level beneath which he could not fall. It was a satisfaction on which to rest," a satisfaction that his straight life before the war had not allowed. On the other hand, he says that when the beast was pressing he did put up resistance, though in vain. As the beast is taking him over ("My brain was sudden and silent as a wild cat, my senses like mud clogging its feet"), his better self tries in vain, to ward it off: "Myself . . . telling the beast it was bad form to spring and vulgar to feed upon the kill. So meshed in nerves and hesitation, it could not be a thing to be afraid of." But his years of guerrilla warfare, he has to admit, mark the triumph of the beast, and his book is the record of that triumph: "It was a real beast, and this book its mangy skin, dried, stuffed and set up squarely for men to stare at."[86]

At Kiswee, just before the capture of Damascus and the

final victory, Lawrence's understanding of his own animality deepens as he looks over the British and Australian regular soldiers that joined forces with the Arab rebels for the final push of the campaign in the desert. He meditates on "the secret of the uniform" and discovers that the wish for degradation is the real driving force of professional soldiers. He sees them as a "crowd, solid, dignified," but he also sees them as "impersonal," separated from life by "death's livery," the uniform they wear. Another trait disjoins them from life—voluntary denial of their humanity: "They had sold their wills and bodies to the state," had submitted to an "abject" service, and in everyman's eye they "were below humanity."

Why would they choose to serve in the military? Lawrence's answer is simple: they wanted degradation, starting with enlistment—the sell-out of the individual to a taskmaster, a sell-out that disqualifies him as a human being: "The soldier assigned his owner the twenty-four hours' use of his body; and sole conduct of his mind and passions." It is true that hunger, thirst for glamour, and the instinct of lawlessness were what induced some soldiers to join up; but "of them all, those only received satisfaction who had sought to degrade themselves, " because in the military they found what they looked for. Lawrence exclaims: "The strange power of war which made us all as a duty to demean ourselves!"

With these words he associates the fate of the soldiers he scans in Kiswee with his own. We do not know if he sought degradation when he first chose to serve in the Middle East. Very probably not. But his having seen degradation in others' lives shows that at this stage of his military career his own depravity haunted him. Lawrence closes his scrutiny of the soldiers with a description in which the adjective "feral" and the references to stench and excrement consign the soldiers to a subhuman world: "And the feral smell of English soldiers: that hot pissy aura of thronged men in woolen clothes: a tart pungency, a breath-catching, ammoniacal; a fervent fermenting naphtha-smell."[87]

Lawrence faces his shame again at an unusual time and place, the moment of his triumph in Damascus, the lodestar. In a scene in which a biographer sees Lawrence's "extreme . . . sense of degradation,"[88] a British major confronts the victorious leader of the Arab Revolt in a hospital filled with unattended wounded and putrefying corpses, and supposing—mistakenly—that Lawrence is responsible for the neglect of both the living and the dead, the major shouts at him: "Scandalous, disgraceful, outrageous, ought to be shot." Lawrence replies, but not with words; he "cackled out like a chicken, with the wild laughter of strain." Contemptuous of Lawrence's irrational response, the major calls him "bloody brute." Lawrence replies with another animal-like sound. "I hooted out again." His utterances and his refusal to speak convince the major that he is dealing with a lesser man, whom he strikes, like the master his recalcitrant beast: "He [the major] smacked me over the face and stalked off." Lawrence passively accepts the unspoken condemnation of the English major, who "left me more ashamed than angry, for in my heart I felt he was right."[89] In other words, the major was right to look upon the victorious leader of the Arab Revolt as an inferior being who deserved to be treated as such.

Though Lawrence knew that the war in the desert had degraded him, he made no effort to regenerate himself in the aftermath of the European conflict. For thirteen years he wasted his talent and energy in the British military—a form of self-enforced degradation. Until a few months before his death, he lived the very kind of life that toward the end of *Seven Pillars of Wisdom* he condemned as degraded. Either the life appealed to him, or he was unable to repel it. The change into a lower form of being did give Lawrence some degree of satisfaction; that is why after the war he clung to the military. But his self-reproach and inhibition kept the beast at bay (perhaps by reminding it that "it was bad form to spring and vulgar to feed upon the kill"); in the private hell of his degradation he lived quietly to the end.

But less inhibited sensibilities and intellects, men who felt contempt for the spiritual or political values of the world in which they lived, were free from the kind of torment that the war and its aftermath brought to Lawrence. They welcomed degradation as a liberating force, as a salutary change for a world in decay. Vorticist Gaudier-Brzeska, who returned to France early in the war, proclaimed that in the trenches of the Western Front he could "gauge the intensity of life."[90] After two months in the trenches the sculptor wrote in *Blast* of admiration for man of the early Stone Age. The primitive spent his life disputing the earth with the animals and hunting for his subsistence; hazardousness and beastliness turned his energy into a "brutal" force and pushed "manhood . . . to its highest potential."

Combat, which for Gaudier-Brzeska was "not a war," but "a murderer hunt" (he remorselessly killed the enemies who refused to surrender), made him happy because it brought him back to the world of primitive man, which would cure the evils of a decayed civilization. It is impossible to know what the regression to savagery would have done to Gaudier-Brzeska's later life because he was killed in 1915. But we know that as late as a few months before his death he still professed enjoyment of the savage life and placed great expectations on it: "I am always in good spirit," he wrote from the trenches, "be it in the mud of the trench or in the warmth of the biwack. I shall come back stronger. . . . It is a good tonic to suffer some discomforts after the very soft life we lead in the towns."[91]

Benito Mussolini, too, valued the beastly life that he and his comrades led in the trenches of Mount Nero in the fall of 1915. "In the morning," he wrote in his diary, "there is no reveille. The soldier sleeps as long as he wishes, and during the day he does nothing. He can go to see friends in other sectors at the risk of being hit by snipers' bullets. . . . He plays cards and gambles, and counts the shots when the gun fires. The distribution of food rations is the only variant in the routine."[92] Mussolini called this life without a sense of time or any useful function, this wait for a wound or for death, this emptiness filled with trivialities, a "natural, primitive life,"[93] which the future leader of Italian Fascism placed above a civilized way of being.

Father Teilhard de Chardin, the French Jesuit who served on the Western Front as a stretcher-bearer, felt that degradation marked the beginning of spiritual regeneration. Like Mussolini, Teilhard de Chardin noted that at the front the quality of life changes; one eats and sleeps when circumstances allow, and sunlight and darkness no longer bear any relationship to the course of life. For Teilhard de Chardin the change the front had brought about meant, not man's fall, but his ascendance above the slavery of daily routine. The preoccupations of health, the family, success, fall away from the soul like a drab garment. Then "the heart makes a new skin," and man, like an explorer or an opium smoker, reaches "new shores." "I need the front," the father confesses, because "I am . . . an explorer."[94]

What is he looking for? On retiring to his dugout in the Chemin des Dames sector one evening in September 1917, he has a vision; he sees "the line taking on the shape of a great Thing," like the result of those "cataclysms" that in remote ages were witnessed by no one else but animals. The "Thing," which represents the waste and decay of the battlefield, is a function of Teilhard de Chardin's degradation but will lead to a future regeneration: "I was," the French Jesuit confesses at the end of his vision, "like a beast in the process of getting a soul."[95]

Gaudier-Brzeska, Mussolini, and Teilhard de Chardin believed that Western civilization was decayed,[96] that war would sweep away the disease, and that the reversion to primitivism would regenerate man. Their individual beliefs perhaps reflected one current of political thought, Italian and French Nationalism, represented by Enrico Corradini and by L'Action Francaise. In Germany, the same kind of beliefs had extraordinary strength, being shaped by the idea of war and conquest as civilizing values.

Thomas Mann thought that the war would bring an end to a world peace that crawled with "spiritual vermin as with worms" and that stank of "the decaying matter of civilization." The German soul, he explained, opposes the "pacifist ideal of civilization, for is not peace an element of civil corruption?"[97] The old idea of von Treitschke and General von Bernhardi that only "the weary, spiritless, and exhausted ages . . . have played with the dream of perpetual peace," and that war "is the greatest factor in the furtherance of culture and power,"[98] took on new life as the war approached. When war began and life in the battlefield sank low, some of the men under the spell of the imperative of war welcomed degradation, and made it an ethical and political value.

Ernst Junger, a youngster from Heidelberg who was soon to be a prolific writer, felt that he had grown up in a society concerned with material values alone, and he yearned for the "great experience." The idea of war intoxicated him, and the Great War, he felt, was his generation's "dream of greatness, power and glory."[99] In 1915 Junger, then a nineteen-year-old lieutenant of the Seventy-third Hanoverian Fusiliers, arrived in the trenches of the chalky hills of Champagne, where an "impervious depression" soon seized him.[100] At the front he lived a "mole's life" for months.

At Les Eparges the fierce French barrage chased him through the trees "like hunted game," and he panted "like a squirrel" as he scurried in search of a hiding place that could not be found; a slight wound sent him dashing "like a bolting horse." Rat-hunts became his favorite pastime in calm periods of trench duty, and a few cats gave him companionship in the dugout. In the beginning, Junger disliked the loneliness and bestiality of the front: "I have a longing for a little warmth and something human," he says.[101] But life at the front has already changed him into a new being, with the confidence and the drive that have so far eluded him on the battlefield. These characteristics will replace his longing for warmth and humanity.

When Junger hears the story about life in an isolated outpost, strewn with corpses and the fatally wounded, under daily barrage and infantry attacks, he, now hardened against emotional pain and fear, shows nothing but "supreme and superhuman indifference."[102] The being that after a few months takes possession of Junger is no longer scared and defensive, as in the first pages of *The Storm of Steel*. The new being acts without fear, ruled by aggressiveness. "You are aquiver with two violent sensations—the tense excitement of the hunter and the terror of the hunted," Junger says of his night patrols in no-man's-land.[103]

Time and experience in the battlefield bring out of him the beast in its lusty pride and murderousness. A frenzy, so intense that he calls it divine, seizes him as he gets ready to go over the top in the last German offensive of the Great War. "Rage, alcohol, and the thirst for blood" push him where "the godlike and the bestial inextricably mingled," where degradation reaches its highest degree. Here Junger reaches a "divine" state of multiple images. It takes the form of the bird ("the overpowering desire to kill winged" his feet), of the werewolf (which "howled and hunted . . . on the track of blood"), and of the savage (the attackers want to take no prisoners, but only to kill, because they are under "the spell of the primeval instinct").[104]

Degradation fascinated Junger at the front, where he came

to understand that he needed it to live the "great experience" he had yearned for at the beginning of the war. Battle, he discovered, gave him the sensation that life had reached its highest pitch,[105] because battle, the struggle for life and death, brought forth in men "the fury of desperate animals."[106] And so he cherished animal fury. Battle was also "like an opiate" to Junger's nerves.[107] When the soldier accustomed to and hardened by violence lives in peace for any length of time, then, deprived of violent shocks, he becomes "worried, unoccupied . . . conscious of a sensation of emptiness." He is left in "a void, the hideous kind of void that follows a demolition"; then "life seems like a roadway between two walls that have collapsed." As the opium addict needs his ration of pipes to feel good, so does the soldier need periodic doses of violence to feel satisfaction with his life. It is "a deterioration," a "descent into hell," but that is what the soldier used to violence wants.[108]

Junger's degradation was more than the compulsion of the soldier for the habitual experience of violence. Junger took drugs both during the war and afterward.[109] The combination of drugs and combat created the kind of addiction that forced him to renew the experience of violence and degradation. Beyond that, Junger valued degradation as the hallmark of the conqueror and the superman. Had not Nietzsche, Junger's favorite author,[110] glorified the "raging of the blond Germanic beast," and the nobility of the "beast of prey, the splendid blonde beast prowling about avidly in search of spoil and victory"? Had not the philosopher imagined a "pack of blond beasts of prey, a conqueror and master race" roaming and terrorizing Europe for centuries, and finally establishing political supremacy on the Continent?[111]

Junger treasured the experience of the beast, which he valued after the war as a political tool that could help the cause of Nationalism. Driven by a burning faith in "Folk and Fatherland," in *Copse 125* Junger urges the triumph of

Nationalism and warns his countrymen that he and war veterans like him would tolerate no opposition. For four long years, he threatens, "we have lived as beasts, not as men. . . . We veterans . . . have become dour. We bite our teeth into ideas as we do into any bit of trench."[112] And in a work symptomatically entitled *Battle as an Inner Experience*, Junger celebrates degradation as the triumph of "the instincts," of the "animalistic tendencies" that lie dormant in man. He wishes for a return to the "red line of primitivity," where the restraint and the humanity wrought by civilization are set aside, where primitive man breaks forth "in all the boundlessness of his unleashed instincts," and where he sings "the song of life": "to live means to kill."[113]

In World War I, the degradation that stunned, lured, and destroyed its victims also repelled them. Critical responses came from writers and soldiers on both the Western and the Italian front. But none of the Italian writers equals the imaginative power of, let us say, Henri Barbusse or Eric Maria Remarque—opponents on the Western Front who fashioned remarkable responses to the withering effect of the front. The response from the Italian line of combat is less forceful.

Attilio Frescura in *Diario di un imboscato* (Diary of a shirker) records two noteworthy observations. A journalist and a minor figure in the world of letters, Frescura saw extensive duty on the Carso and Asiago plateaus and on the river Piave as an infantry lieutenant. But the diary describes his reactions to events he observed behind the front line, not on the battlefield itself. The first occasion is the sight of a regiment marching in stiff, mechanical fashion past civilian authorities on the parade ground. The performance shows how military discipline can change man. Frescura thinks of the innate dignity and strength of man, and refuses to believe that the change he is witnessing can ever occur. Yet six thousand soldiers before his eyes acting like so many automatons convince him that they are beings other than human.

Frescura believes that the soldiers could not have been changed into what they are if they had in truth been men to start with. So he concludes that, paradoxically, they were never really men. "Men, a formidable force, can be taken away from their homes, from their women, from their affairs. Men, who are a formidable force, are forced into a ditch on which other men pour shells and explosives that tear both men and ditch apart. . . . Men, a formidable force, are lined up 'by four,' are marched on the beat, 'one, two, one, two,' massed, locked to one another. . . . Man, a formidable force, is like an ox. Strong and stupid".[114]

The adventures of a boy at the front prompt Frescura to reflect again on degradation, and to represent its victims as responding mildly, with a twinge of conscience. In September 1916 the military police picks up a boy, dressed like a soldier and apparently lost, in the rear of the battlefield on the Carso. Twelve-year-old Muraro Menotti from Udine tells the officer who interrogates him that he joined up at the beginning of the war, and now belongs to a regiment of the Chieti brigade. He has lived with the soldiers in the trenches of the Carso, of Monfalcone, and of the hottest spot on the lower Isonzo front, Mount San Michele. The boy, blondish, lean, with a roguish look, surprises his listener with the precision and frankness of his answers, and with his quiet boldness. "So, you have made war," the officer comments when he hears of Muraro's precocious military career. "Yessir," answers the boy.

> "Do you like to make war?"
> "Yessir."
> "Have you ever fired?"
> "By God, haven't I!"

"A rifle?"

"Yessir. They taught me to keep my legs
wide apart to withstand the recoil."

"Have you killed any Austrians?"

"Who know? In the trenches, you know, sometimes one shoots without seeing anything."

"And what do you want to do now?"

"I'll stick around some regiment until I find my own, the Ninth Infantry. That's my regiment. Everybody knows me there."

"But does your father know that you are in the war?"

"Yessir, and he is happy."

"And your mother?"

"Eh, my mother, no. You know, women are all the same. . . . "

"Then we will send you back to your mother."

The boy, who stands rigid at attention, looks around with wide-open eyes, understands that the threat is real, and breaks into tears, sobbing desperately. So the officer allows Muraro to hang around Frescura's unit.[115]

Frescura, struck by the boy's love of war, danger and violence, muses that Muraro, "like the animals that take on the color of the environment in which they live," has taken on "the soul" of his surroundings, the front. The boy's stay with Frescura's unit shows what kind of "soul" the front has given him. He drinks wine while playing cards in the taverns with the soldiers, and when drunk he beats up his contemporaries and even their mothers. In the end Muraro, who "swears very well, shouts and quarrels like a grown-up soldier," is sent home to his mother. He is sent away, not because he is a troublemaker, but because his behavior upsets the conscience of the troops around him.

They find the degenerate behavior of Muraro, a boy who still bears the physical features of a child, intolerable. The adults, confronted by the conspicuousness of degradation in a being whose essence is innocence, flinched and got rid of the boy. "It was wrong," Frescura concludes, "to believe that he who loves adventure, risk, and war, he who has no horror of the dead and of the wounded, who has no fear of the trenches and who despises life, could also have the gracefulness and gentleness of the children who are afraid of the dark." Although Muraro is still a few years from manhood, he is already a special kind of man, one whose real essence could be perceived only if he had "tusks, some hair, and a tail."[116]

Tension, drama, and social consciousness characterize Henri Barbusse's response to degradation in *Le feu (Under Fire)*. Battle changes the men of Barbusse's squad; the beast seizes them, but it fails to conquer their spirit. The alienation from humanity that they suffer sets the stage for their renewal. At the climax of action in *Under Fire,* the French squad aggressively attacks the International Trench, without fear. As the soldiers advance through no-man's-land, they stop for a moment and look at one another, discovering that "fever" burns in their eyes, that their cheekbones have become blood red and their breathing has turned into snorting, while their hearts pound in their bodies. The physical changes prefigure a moral change. The death of their lieutenant makes them hesitate, but the frenzy that has worked their bodies up translates into collective boldness: "Forward! Go on, go on," the men incite one another. In a hail of bullets, they hurl themselves into an endless race "toward the horizon." The sight of German helmets bobbing in the trenches casts a spell on the French, who plunge ahead robot-like: "bent rigidly forward, almost incapable of turning [their heads] to right or to left." Finally, "driven as by the wind," the French overrun the German trench.[117] The soldiers again stop and look at one another, but this time Barbusse is unable to recognize any of his comrades: "There is some change working in them. A frenzied excitement is driving them all out of themselves." They are endowed with inhuman daring. The strange, unexpected strength the French found in themselves during the assault drives them to conquer yet another German trench. The new attack accentuates the transformation that the first onslaught had caused; nothing can be seen in the soldiers but "what is inflamed, blood-red with sweat, eyes flashing." The men move on, "elated, immensely confident, ferocious."[118]

Flushed with victory, Corporal Bertrand prides himself on having killed three of the enemy who refused to surrender, striking them down "like a madman." At this point, with no more Germans in sight and no more killing to be done, the frenzy that drove the French soldiers subsides, and they realize that they have conquered because of what they have become. "We were all like beasts when we got here!" Corporal Bertrand tells himself and his comrades. They realize that their exploits have turned them into "domestic beasts" and "murderers . . . hard and persistent murderers."[119]

The French soldiers' response to degradation breaks the code of the realistic novel to which Barbusse has so far adhered,[120] thereby paving the way for the surfacing idealism. After yet another attack, idealism finds expression in the last pages of the novel, which air Barbusse's humanistic and socialistic goals, "the entente among the multitudes, the uplifting of the people of the world." Barbusse's highest standard is born out of the soldiers' yearning for redemption from the evil that has made them beasts—namely, militarism. "The work of the future will be to wipe out the present . . . like something abominable and shameful. . . . Shame on military glory, shame on armies, shame on the soldier's calling, that changes men by turns into stupid victims or ignoble brutes."[121]

Like Barbusse's soldiers, Paul Baumer, the protagonist of *All Quiet on the Western Front*, descends into the hell of degradation, but unlike Barbusse's protagonists, whose fall sparks belief in regeneration and the strength to struggle for it, Baumer meets in degradation the evil that denies life. Unable to shake free from depravity because he knows that his physical survival depends on it, Baumer becomes its unwilling victim, who dies even before the gun kills him. Baumer grew up in the same country as Junger did but unlike the storm trooper who looks for and finds in the war the "great experience," Baumer enters the war out of a sense of duty. Standing at the periphery of the German culture that fired Junger with consuming belligerency, Baumer merely bends to its dictates. He joins up only after prodding by Kantorek, his high school teacher, and by the community, which regards any young man lukewarm about fighting as a coward. A dutiful German, he plays the role that his fatherland has assigned; he "loved" his country and "went courageously into every action." The reality of the war, however, depresses him more than the moral imperative exalts him, and he quickly learns that if "duty to one's country is the greatest thing . . . death-throes are stronger."[122] At the front, Baumer's simple but quick mind understands that the soldier who changes into an animal has a better chance of survival, but he will also discover that if animality saves his skin—at least for a time—it will diminish him as a man over the years. Since animality keeps him alive, he clings to it; but in robbing him of his humanity, beastliness also repels him. The tension that pervades Remarque's novel grows out of the conflict between Baumer's struggle to survive physically, on the one hand, and his realization that this struggle robs him of humanity, on the other.

At the beginning of the novel, Baumer and his comrades, already veterans of the war, appear to be degenerates. Having come back from the front line for a rest, they are "satisfied and at peace" from having eaten well, not because of having earned a victory or a medal: "Now our bellies are full of beef and haricot beans. . . . Each man has another mess-tin full for the evening; and, what is more, there is double ration of sausage and bread." The satisfaction of physical needs is of great importance to these soldiers; it replaces the inner strength needed to endure a living death, a strength that has vanished: "But our comrades are dead, we cannot help them, they have their rest—and who knows what is waiting for us? We will make ourselves comfortable and sleep, and eat as much as we can stuff into our bellies and drink and smoke so that the hours are not wasted. Life is short."[123] In a world where human values are crumbling, relief from fear, pain, and death comes from those comforts that satisfy man and animal alike.

Baumer and his comrades transform themselves easily into lower beings because the army has prepared them well for the change before they reached the front. During military training they saw that authority kills the best in man—intelligence, education, and culture. "We have learned," Baumer recalls, "that a bright button is weightier than four volumes of Schopenhauer. . . . We recognized that what matters is not the mind but the boot brush, not intelligence but the system, not freedom but the drill." He has also learned that the authority of a mere corporal influences him more than the dictates of his parents, teachers, and "the whole gamut of culture from Plato to Goethe."[124] During military training he undergoes what Rudolf Binding called "a classic reversion to the primitive—a perversion."[125] Baumer discovers early what T.E. Lawrence found out at the end of a war—that submission to military discipline is "renunciation of personality such as one would not have asked of the meanest servant."[126]

But the training gives Baumer and his comrades also the means of physical survival—the toughness of animals: "We became hard," he recognizes, "suspicious, pitiless, vicious, tough. . . . Had we gone into the trenches without this period of training most of us would certainly have gone mad. We did not break down but endured. . . . By the animal instinct that is awakened in us we are led and protected." When bullets and bombs fly, that instinct tells the soldiers where to run, when to duck, and when to hit the ground. The instinct of the animal takes over as soon as the soldier faces the enemy: "We march up, moody or good-tempered soldiers—we reach the zone where the front begins and become on the instant human animals. . . . We turn into animals when we go up to the line, because that is the only thing which brings us through safely. . . . We want to live at any price."[127]

But survival exacts an exorbitant price that makes life itself worthless. Baumer begins to understand the price of survival in chapter 6 of the twelve-chapter novel, as well as in the section containing the famous metaphor "the front is a cage."[128] While Baumer and his comrades cower in the dugout during an endless artillery barrage, in rushes a swarm of "corpse-rats" with "shocking, evil, naked faces" and "nude tails," which have already "bitten to death and devoured two large cats and a dog." Invaded by the rats, the soldiers forget about the barrage, whose blast "is like a blow from the paw of a raging beast of prey," and instead fight furiously against the rats: "Torches light up. . . . Everyone yells and curses and slaughters. . . . Faces are distorted, arms strike out, the beasts scream; we just stop in time to avoid attacking one another."[129] In warding off the rats, the soldiers struggle against the impending disintegration of their own humanity. The assault by the corpse-rats, animals that feed on human bodies, aptly represents the depth and the ugliness of the decay that devours the soldiers.

As the Germans retreat under the French infantry attack that follows the barrage, degradation gradually conquers them. The description of their ruin blends dehumanization ("thugs, murderers"), animality ("cats") and struggle for survival: "We have become wild beasts. We do not fight, we defend ourselves against annihilation . . . No longer do we lie helpless, awaiting [death] on the scaffold, we can destroy and kill, to save ourselves. . . . Crouching like cats we run on, overwhelmed by this wave that bears us along, that fills us with ferocity, turning us into thugs, into murderers . . . this wave that multiplies our strength with fear and madness and greed of life, seeking and fighting for nothing but our deliverance." These Germans fight fiercely but unheroically; Remarque avoids calling them soldiers; he calls them "men," more precisely "dead men." But they are very much alive, for their bodies, impelled by the animal, move vigorously; what is dead in these men is their souls.

When the fighting dies down, Baumer and his comrades temporarily regain their humanity; they "gradually . . . become something like men again." Yet they are not quite men, for as soon as the retreat ends, their thoughts turn to food ("the corned beef over there is famous along the whole front. . . . We have a constant hunger"), to the satisfaction of animal needs. When they have secured jam, cognac, turnips, five tins of corned beef, and a thin loaf of white bread, they settle down for a big meal, again feeding their belief in the value of physical safety. The eating scene mingles the fulfillment of physical needs with that of the animal's highest purpose, survival: "It is a good thing we have something decent to eat at last; we still have a use for all our strength. Enough to eat is just as valuable as a good dugout; it can save our lives; that is the reason we are so greedy for it."[130]

In the end, physical survival becomes meaningless to Baumer as he realizes that the front has robbed him of his soul, and that life devoid of inner self makes no sense. Almost every battle signals alienation and the irretrievability of the German soldier's former self ("We turn into animals when we go up to the line. . . so we turn into wags and loafers when we are out resting. We can do nothing else, it is sheer necessity"). After the successful retreat described in chapter 6, Baumer's imagination evokes serene scenes of home life, and the soldier suddenly feels that a barrier has grown up between his prewar life and his present one. He longs for the simple, natural life of his memories, while realizing that what he longs for can never be recaptured. It will elude him not because of death or wounds, but because the spirit that once felt the beauty of that life is now dead. In the trenches the scenes of past life "are completely lost to us," Baumer reflects, "and they stand remote on the horizon, they are an apparition, a mysterious reflection drawing us home, that we fear and love without hope. They are strong and our desire is strong —but they are unattainable, and we know it, . . . [we] are lost" and "dead."[131]

Even toward the end of *All Quiet on the Western Front*, Baumer clings to the value of physical survival ("as in a polar expedition, every expression of life must serve only the preservation of existence. . . . That is the only way to save ourselves" in the trenches). He finally realizes, however, that the effort to ensure physical survival has led to spiritual death. Life at the front "has transformed us into unthinking animals in order to give us the weapon of instinct," Baumer says of himself and his comrades; at the same time, he recognizes, it has lent us "the indifference of wild creatures." When the sinister meaning of the transformation becomes clear, then what Bertrand Russell called "secret shame" seizes Baumer. He and his comrades have become beastly through the deliberate perversion of life's purpose. In civilian life man strives to improve himself, but in war he strives for debasement: "Our inner forces are not exerted toward regeneration, but toward degeneration. The Bushmen are primitive and naturally so, but we are primitive in an artificial sense, and by virtue of the utmost effort." The deliberate perversion heightens the soldiers' consciousness of their depravity and introduces a crisis ("unexpectedly a flame of grievous and terrible yearning flares up"). When the crisis comes for Baumer, he splits in two, and like the dual selves of T.E. Lawrence in the desert of Arabia, Baumer's are set up one against the other like two strangers, in a dialogue without mutual understanding. One self is the human being that once lived but has now lost his reality, while the present being is animal-like and barely comprehends his former life: "In the quiet hours when the puzzling reflection of former days, like a blurred mirror, projects beyond me the figure of my present existence, I often sit over against myself, as before a stranger, and wonder how the unnameable active principle that calls itself Life has adapted itself even to this form."[132] Life has adapted itself by destroying the former being, leaving only "this form" of life, which is merely existence.

Remarque's fictional portrayal of spiritual death unredeemed by physical survival is faithfully reflected in the correspondence of a young German who was in fact a soldier. It took the student Franz Blumenfeld, a private from Freiburg, neither much time nor a novelist's imagination to understand that to fight and survive he had to give up his humanity. But he also understood that physical survival does not matter when all else dies. In October 1914 Blumenfeld wrote to his parents, who were eager to send him a bulletproof vest, that neither wounds nor death frightened him. Rather, he feared a "great spiritual loneliness," the gradual loss of "faith in human nature . . . in all that is good in the world," a loss that for him was harder to bear than the hunger, cold, and danger in the trenches. He was afraid of becoming a brute: "One thing weighs upon me more from day to day—the fear of getting brutalized." Although Blumenfeld was more patriotic than Baumer, and although he believed that "what counts is . . . readiness to make a sacrifice," he showed no willingness to sacrifice his soul at the front; he preferred death to a soulless life. "What is the good of escaping all the bullets and shells, if my soul is injured?"[133] Blumenfeld turned down the offer of the bullet-proof vest, thereby signifying that he chose death over meaningless life. Like Paul Baumer, Blumenfeld died on the battlefield on the Western Front.

2. A Bath of Black Blood

A subtle and cultivated malaise, a kind of degradation wholly different from the savagery that seizes man on the battlefield, appeared in Europe before World War I. Degradation on the battlefield, we have seen, destroys man's spirit but enhances his fighting ability, thereby giving the combatant an advantage. The sense of decay that characterized some European countries before the war offered one political advantage: it bent people to the will of their leaders and to the requirements of war. Three members of the generation of 1914—two real and one fictional—show how the malaise drew men and nations into war.

The brilliant critic Renato Serra, called up in April 1915, within that same month was marching toward the Italian-Austrian border, and from the Tagliamento River he wrote that he supported the war then being waged and that war in general was "necessary."[1] When Serra was killed on the slopes of Mount Podgora in July, he, like other patriots and intellectuals of his generation who embraced war, might have appeared to die for the love and glory of his country. But after the war the publication of Serra's *Esame di coscienza di un letterato* (Self-scrutiny of a man of letters), written before its author went to the front, gave a different meaning to Serra's death and support of the war. When Benedetto Croce in his *History of Italy* reminisced about the life and work of the critic, he smelled decadence and wrote that Serra had fought because war gave him "a voluptuous quiver."[2] Other scholars echoed Croce's view, stating that it was both a life-denying impulse and a submission to the "instinct of the herd" that drove the writer from Cesena into the war.[3]

Besides supporting these views, the *Self-scrutiny* reveals a surprising indifference to human values. Neither war in general nor the Great War in particular, Serra wrote, made any sense. The conflict that had engulfed all of Europe would in the end bring "no transformation and no renewal" to the peoples who had fought the battles. Some, he predicted, would be tired and others would be unsettled, but the fundamentals of life would be unaltered. War, he concluded, "changes nothing, improves nothing"; it "neither changes nor creates artistic values" and it affects "nothing in the moral universe," neither the "spirit of our civilization" nor the course of history.[4]

Serra conceded that the Great War might free the oppressed, punish the oppressors, and bring a degree of justice to some nations. But for him the conflict would still be meaningless, because nothing could relieve the anguish of the wounded dying alone on the battlefield or compensate for the blood and pain of the survivors.[5]

Although Serra understood the absurdity and cruelty of war, he conceived of man, including himself, as worthless. He believed that "egoism" rules life, degrades man, and "feeds the vitality of the herd." Man's blind attachment to his small patch of land, to his cravings, to his work—even to his suffering— wrote Serra, have demeaned humanity and made of it a herd of animals. Wars have come and gone, devastating lands and terrorizing men, but humans, unmindful of evil destiny, cling to their worthless lives. Their "instinctive and primordial animality" allows for no improvement: "Each one of these innumerable and tenacious creatures . . . continues to plow his furrow, to tread upon the same path, to make children on the same plot of land that covers his dead. When he is interrupted, he begins all over; when he is chased away, he returns."[6]

Serra concluded his *Self-scrutiny* with the image of himself marching to war in the company of the masses he despised: "I am glad we will travel the same road together . . . to march, to stop, to rest . . . together," like a herd.[7] Why would he, an intellectual and an esteemed member of society, want to mix with the populace, who would contaminate him by their baseness? The answer is that Serra wanted to efface himself, wanted death because he felt that he, like his people, was degenerate. He looked on war as the best opportunity to end a worthless life. Death through war had already beckoned to him in 1911 when in Cesena he had watched a group of recruits preparing to leave to fight in Libya. Serra saw in the young soldiers the same malady that in 1915 would fascinate him and lead him to war and death: the "dark, hot, blind impulse that since the beginning of the world leads one man to follow another: the aimless, impersonal, irrational, eternal, and beastly force of the masses."[8] By 1915 he was ready to merge with the "beastly force of the masses," yearning "to live and to die together [with the soldiers] without knowing the reason for it."[9] Almost as if Serra had wished for punishment of the "instinctive primordial animality" of peoples and individuals, he embraced war and its absurdity.

Filippo Rubè, the protagonist of Borgese's novel *Rubè*, encountered earlier, epitomizes the crisis of men who, like Renato Serra, lost their sense of human worth and chose war to rescue themselves from their tormented minds. A persistent but elusive malaise troubles the thirty-year-old lawyer from southern Italy. He diagnoses his despondence as a sickness of the soul, as the symptom of an inscrutable guilt, and he calls it "shameful." He searches for a cure, which he seems to find in the submission of his being to the domination of the body: "I will put the body, which is healthy, in charge of my sick soul," he decides. Believing that the soldier lives by his physical self alone, he enlists: "I will live the military life, which is mostly physical, and my soul will be reborn." In the train on his way to the front, his personality dissolves and he feels better, as if he were inhaling "opium smoke." He is confident that he will be regenerated because he has rid himself of his responsibilities toward himself and toward others. He is relieved of the burden of making decisions—he need only obey and serve—because he has finally found "redemption from the serfdom of need" by giving up his free will. Above all, he believes that "war, the healer of the world," will prove to be the medicine that wipes out his malaise. "I am a man without distinction," Rubè acknowledges, but he at once reassures himself that "war uplifts me." As the lieutenant falls asleep on the seat of the train speeding away from Rome toward the front, he perceives war as "admirable in its divine necessity and purifying splendor."[10]

None of Rubè's expectations come true. Life at the front shows him instead that all war does is to give men like himself, men "without tomorrow," the chance "to get rid of themselves." He concludes that nothing but a frenzy of self-destruction drives men to war. But, clinging to the idea of war's regenerating power, he contrives to get wounded and to feel "the joy of being in death's orbit without trembling."[11] By feeding his illusion that war will rescue him, this artificial bravery only worsens his disease. When Rubè returns to civilian, but not normal, life, he cowardly lets his mistress Celestina drown in stormy Lake Maggiore. In the end, he is killed on the street in the midst of a political demonstration while he extols both Fascism and Communism, as well as the soulless life of man as a herd member: "We will all be [under Fascism or Communism] in a big barracks, all equal and all nameless."[12] Rubè had reached the depths of incurable decay.

Like fictional Rubè, Pierre Drieu La Rochelle, Parisian poet and novelist, marched to war in search of renewal. In retrospect he looked on the time in the army as "the most satisfying" of his life; he described World War I as his "last hope of salvation."[13] He had spent his childhood and adolescence tormented by an inferiority complex. His mother denied the boy emotional support, while his father often excoriated and mocked the youth's fragility by extolling manliness and bravery and implying that his son's worst fault was cowardice. His father's censure and carping told young Drieu clearly that he was an inferior being, a degenerate. "I feared him," Drieu wrote of his father, "with the cowardly tenderness of a slave who secretly cherished his master." The mother overprotected the boy, and confirmed his degeneration by keeping him "captive" until he reached fifteen. The boy "felt a pusillanimous and domesticated bourgeois female," a "little slave."[14]

In 1913, the twenty-year-old Drieu was drafted into the army, where his sense of inferiority intensified. He kept apart from his fellow recruits and from the officers because he felt less than a man. He was ashamed of himself; he felt "a nobody, a nonentity, something completely empty, a spineless funk, less than a spineless funk, a nothing." By the time the war broke out he had fallen so low that he "wanted to efface by death the too weak being" that he thought he was.[15] But war was to give him the illusion of being saved.

On a sunny morning in August 1914, Private Drieu and his company faced the German lines in the trenches of Charleroi, inside the Belgian border. That morning he looked on his comrades as "peasants" and projected onto them his own depravity: "Nearly all these farmers [were] alcoholics, degenerates, and weaklings." He saw himself as an animal in the midst of a herd, "a branded calf among ten million other calves and oxen" waiting to be slaughtered. But Drieu suddenly vaulted from the depths of gloom to the heights of euphoria after a French platoon mistakenly started firing on his company. When nobody else made a move to stop the shooting, Drieu, as if "suddenly released by a spring," approached the company commander and offered to do what no others dared. As he ran into the open and bullets whistled around him, he rejoiced at separating himself from the other soldiers, from a mass of mediocrity incapable of following the heroic impulse.[16] He thought that he was shedding the burden he had carried all his young life, thereby regenerating himself. Drieu, however, was mistaken; he had only exchanged moral paralysis for another kind of degeneration—savagery.

Drieu fought for no cause, no ideal. "Why do we fight?" he asked, answering, "for fighting's sake. . . . We have no aim." War transmuted his sense of inferiority into an irrational, savage energy that on the battlefield exploded into what he believed to be ennobling behavior. "We screamed," he wrote about another of his military exploits, a bayonet charge at Charleroi. "We howled like beasts. We were beasts. Who leapt and shouted? The beast that is inside man, the beast that is the very life of man. The beast that makes love, war and revolution."[17] Drieu became a devotee of the cult of violence, which he equated with manhood. "I am no pacifist," he proclaimed after Charleroi, "I loathe an unmanly man, a man unable to assert himself with his body, or to suffer with it. . . . For me, man cannot stop being a warrior."[18] Drieu went so far as to side with the master practitioners of violence, becoming a Nazi collaborator during World War II. In March 1945, when he found out that the liberators had ordered his arrest, he killed himself.

Serra, who went to war in a fatalistic mood; Rubè, who served in the expectation of salvation; and Drieu, who took up arms with indifference—each discovered violence to be uplifting. What the three had in common was a sense of degradation. Had they not regarded themselves as degraded beings, war would have had no appeal. It rarely pays to dwell upon individual human experiences that end in failure, but Serra, Rubè, and Drieu shared a destiny that transcended the individual. Each of these three lives is a microcosm of a world pulled toward war by sickness and decay. National decay became a reason for war in the same way that personal decay impelled individuals to take to the battlefield. Among the European nations, Italy was unique in the way it felt the burden of national decay and the pull toward war. Intellectuals and politicians in Italy eagerly sought proof of public decay, even resorting to fabrication. They flung the tell-tale signs at the people, prodding them to war.

A few months before Italy entered the war, Benedetto Croce turned his attention to the pro-war arguments of the interventionists. In the article "Undeserved Fortunes," he urged the country to stay out of the European conflict because Italy was unprepared to wage war. Croce called for military restraint because he believed that if Italy entered the war and won without making real sacrifices, the victory would do more harm than good to the country. He feared not that unpreparedness would lead to the waste of lives or to defeat, but that victory obtained through the efforts of others would hand the Italian people unearned military and political gains, leaving them, as in the aftermath of the Risorgimento, to lie back in their "habitual inertia and indiscipline" and lose even the self-confidence needed for the ordinary business of living. But the Neapolitan philosopher urged Italy to prepare for and enter a war in which the Italian people would have to fight and bleed in earnest, so that their suffering would improve the moral tone of national life. He accepted the interventionists' argument that Italy had become a nation through foreign help and that it had to pay a price for its undeserved fortune. If Italy kept out of the war, the country would show again its helplessness, and when others had fought the war, it would find itself "morally weaker" than it had been at the beginning. Croce saw in the Great War the opportunity for Italy both to get rid of its sense of inferiority, of the "reproaches of our conscience that generate insecurity and degradation in our political and social life," and to "expiate its guilt."[19]

When the war on the Italian front was more than two years old, Croce returned to the theme of Italian failure in the Risorgimento, calling it cowardice. Cowardice, he wrote, was a long-standing vice among Italians; it dated back to the fall of the Roman Empire, and it became glaring at the end of the fifteenth century, when the Italians failed to oppose the French invasion of the peninsula. That failure earned the Italians an international reputation for cowardice. Time and again after Charles VIII's invasion in 1494, both the French and the Germans charged the Italians with cowardice. But now, Croce wrote in September 1917, the Italian army fights Austria and Germany to accomplish "nothing less than . . . to redeem definitively the Italian people from a fifteen-centuries-old guilt." Even if through war the Italian people were to gain only the strength "to look with unbowed head at the peoples of the world as equals," this alone would be of "immense moral and political benefit."[20]

Trento and Trieste, the "unredeemed" lands and the sacred goals of Italian nationalism, were only a pretext, "the fools' motive," wrote Paolo Marconi, one of the fallen Italian officers whose life and thoughts are immortalized in Adolfo Omodeo's *Momenti della vita di guerra*. For Marconi, the real aim of the war was to wipe out the shame bequeathed by the Risorgimento to the present generation. The Risorgimento could not be viewed as a political success because only a minority of Italians, not the people as a whole, strove for liberty and unity, because it was good fortune and the foreigner, rather than Italy's own resources, that helped to achieve liberty and unity, and because the achievements were "insufficiently bathed in blood." Comparing the achievements of the Italians with those of other European peoples in the nineteenth century, Marconi saw that the

Risorgimento was a "shame." The French had bled to assert man's rights, and the Germans had fought "single-handledly and tenaciously" since Luther to show the world what a "great people" they were. But the Italians, Marconi regretted, had lain idle and created nothing: "no religion, no country . . . no honor." Worse yet, they "have sold themselves out" and they are "dishonored, enslaved." We want now, Marconi concluded, something more important than Trento and Trieste; we want "to redeem . . . Italy."[21]

Marconi's historical perspective differed from Croce's: the officer of the Alpine Corps reached back only to the Risorgimento, whereas Croce searched beyond the Renaissance. Nonetheless, both the philosopher and the soldier extracted from the past the same prescription for the present: something had gone terribly wrong with the Italian people in their quest for nationhood and what was needed to repair the damage was to make war.

In the years just preceding the outbreak of World War I, many Italian politicians and intellectuals agreed that the country had not worked or suffered enough to earn its unity, beyond which the people had made little economic and social progress. Such thinking grew out of the disillusionment generated by extravagant ambitions that had gone unfulfilled, out of the "complex world-ruling romanism absurdly disproportionate to both the modern world and modern Italy." The seeds were the disappointment that Italy had failed to become a great military power or the center of the European commonwealth, and the delusion that the Italian people, "a people elect, a redeemer," had betrayed its mission as "a ruler of the world."[22] Politicians and intellectuals alike contributed to creating and exploiting the "terrible sickness,"[23] the belief that the Italian people were not what they ought to be. The exploiters fixed blame, turning a past that had its moments of glory and beauty into a source of dissatisfaction and collective guilt. They pointed to decadence and vice, perceived or conjured up, they turned the image of a fallen people into an instrument of war. As Eugenio Garin noted, through their "tragic irresponsibility . . . criminal will . . . and foolish rhetoric"[24] they held up war and destruction as uplifting goals.

The nationalists charged the Italian people with egoism, but Enrico Corradini, the nationalist leader, found egoism thriving only among the opponents of war. The policy of nonintervention, he proclaimed, is the product of those who call war frightening, immoral, and barbarous because they know, or fear, that war might interfere with the realization of their "material egoist interests." For Corradini, such interests kill all generous impulses. Only generous men, those who know how to overcome their "personal material egoism," can understand that war is "desirable and holy" because it brings death, and death welds the individual to the nation. Corradini thus urged his selfish compatriots to fight, to die, and to redeem themselves. "By devoting himself to death the insignificant egotist helps to create the life of the true great individual—the fatherland." Fought for this purpose, Corradini concluded, war "is supremely moral and supremely civil."[25]

The accusation of egoism came from other quarters as well. Luigi Russo, an instructor at the military academy in Caserta in 1917 and later a prominent literary critic, thought that the concern with "personal egoistic advantages" weighed down the "ethical life" of the Italian people. He extolled the army as a "national educational institution" capable of curing the egoism that generated "civic analphabetism," that is, disrespect for authority, self-seeking, and reluctance to sacrifice "material advantages."[26] Some of the men who had known the cruel danger of the front felt the same as the professor speaking in the safety of the classroom. War may bring Italy no political gains, the gallant nobleman Ignazio di Trabia wrote from the front. It may even give free rein to the murderous instinct, yet war will give the people a considerable advantage by killing "egoism in all its shapes."[27]

In 1914 Giovanni Boine, who wrote for *La voce*, the periodical founded in 1908 in Florence to deal with "the problems of public life" and to help reinvigorate Italian culture and politics,[28] saw the Italians in the throes of an "egoistic torpor." To them the notion of the fatherland meant nothing; they cared only about success in their personal affairs, gains in social security, universal voting rights, and a steady income from their bank deposits. These petty concerns and aspirations masked something graver than egoism: "a profound sickness . . . a spiritual gangrene hidden in everybody's soul." Boine was convinced that the disease sooner or later would lead either to civil war or to the enslavement of Italy by the foreigner. He felt the need for "a common enthusiasm" capable of "tearing each individual violently away from himself," something as compelling as the birth of a new religion or, even better, war, to generate the enthusiasm that would suppress egoism.[29] Boine's indictment of Italian egoism carried an authority that was missing in other writers because the *vociano* drew on Hegel's idea that egoism—concern for personal rights and "right in things . . . gain, enjoyment"—represented a distinct peril to national life, a peril to be removed by any means.[30]

Both Boine's *Discorsi military* (Military discourses) and Russo's *Vita e disciplina militare* (Military life and discipline) found in the military discipline of war the cure for selfishness, a national disease. Military life, with its demands for sacrifice and suffering, Russo wrote, would give the citizen a "highly moral" education and build in him a civic and national "sentiment."[31] The supreme form of egoism, in his view, was the reluctance of the Italian people to do battle. Combat, he wrote in a chapter entitled "Ideal Eternity of War," means progress, while peace equals stagnation. "War, or simply struggle, is intrinsic to human reality. . . . All life is struggle, all history is struggle: even the life of the individual is a perennial struggle against himself." It follows that "outside of this struggle there is nothing but rot, dissolution, and death." Russo conveniently disregarded the bloodless struggles of individuals and nations to better their spiritual and material life, and even when he acknowledged the grief and death, he icily dismissed them as mere "formal" manifestations that do not cast doubts on the ideal nature of war.[32] Boine, too, gave war a philosophical slant by injecting into it an "ideal" and "eternal" meaning: "The history of the world is . . . [the] history of its wars. . . . Nations vie and struggle one against the other in the same way as individuals fight among themselves in society."[33]

As one of the leaders of intellectual life in Italy on the eve of the Great War, Benedetto Croce helped lead his country to war. He shaped, as we have seen, the Italian nation's reputation for egoism and worthlessness, and then assigned to war the redeeming role. "Life is . . . a ruthless struggle," he wrote in January 1915, five months before Italy plunged into conflict, and war is the law that governs the struggle. History itself proves the validity of this law, for history is nothing but a procession of wars and violent acts. Croce warned the Italians: "Woe on the peoples who refuse to take part in the struggle, woe on the neuters, woe on the men with 'clean hands.' "[34]

Croce's belief in war was so strong that the extraordinary number of casualties and economic losses in the European conflict failed to shake it. When in 1919 he was asked his opinion of the League of Nations, the international body created to help resolve controversies and head off conflicts, the philosopher answered that such effort was futile because it sought to implement a "mechanistic" ideal of equality and peace. Conflicts among nations, he reminded the interviewer, cannot be stopped, as they are the very "spring of history and reality." Besides, he added, it would be unfortunate if conflicts were in fact to cease, since utter boredom would then engulf the world.

After the armistice, Croce seemed to show a glimmer of humanity. In November 1918 he refused to join other Italians in celebrating victory because Italy "comes out of the war as a man emerges from a serious and deadly disease."[35] As is well known, Croce admired Germany because he believed that Kant and Hegel had given the world the best in philosophy. His germanophilia went as far as extolling one of Germany's crudest advocates of violence—von Treitschke.[36] Croce's refusal to celebrate the Italian victory may thus have had more to do with the philosopher's sorrow for the defeat of a beloved nation than with the suffering that war had brought to Italy.

Croce's view of war as a moral and historical imperative was reflected with shrill extremism in Futurism, the artistic and intellectual movement that sprang up before World War I. The Futurists differed from Croce only in philosophizing less and writing with more cynicism and brutality. "Springtime, youth, heroism, revolution, progress, and civilization"—which Croce's scholarly mind would place under the heading of "history and reality"—in fact "worship human blood" and thrive on destruction, wrote Filippo Marinetti, the leader of Futurism. "Savage and ruthless instincts" drive the "most vigorous" people, the kind that determine the course of history. The other category of humans, dull, tired, or old, believe in goodness, in the purity of ideas and feelings, in love for humanity, and in "other abstractions" intended to bring about peace and happiness—but such people do nothing.[37] If the future of the world belongs to the strong and the ruthless, then the Italian people have no future. In Giovanni Papini's words, they lead a "mediocre and trite" life, bound by the fetters of custom, by laziness, and by routine. They feel no urge to "do something important," so that their life may take on some meaning and some beauty. These are the people whose worthlessness caused Papini to conclude that "the Italian soul is mean."[38]

Even some contributors to *La voce* wrote with unmistakable Futurist spirit; and Papini was one of them. The conclusions he drew about the worthlessness of the common man in Italy at the beginning of the war had their genesis in the meditations of his famous intellectual biography of 1912, *Un uomo finito* (*A* finished man). Early in his life, Papini says in *Un uomo finito,* he became convinced that men—which to Papini meant Italian men—are either "crooks" or "morons." He felt, therefore, contempt for all average men, for "those I knew and for those I had never known, for those who blamed me and for those who acclaimed me, for those who helped me and for those who shunned me." As life around him nauseated him more and more, he determined to make every man feel his own nausea and to pull him out of his "barbarous and savage life." He set out to redeem mediocrity, to turn average men into real men. He did it with a peculiar style. "I made them realize that they were beasts. To show my interest in them, I beat them up. If I stooped to them, I did it to better whip them and to amuse myself. I whipped them while showing them how cowardly they lived out their life, how low their desires were, how primitive their ideas were, how great their ignorance and their inability to reason straight were."[39] In 1915 the hand of destiny came to Papini's aid: Italy went to war, and the rage of the gun would carry out the intent of the intellectual.

For other members of *La voce's* circle the Italian soul was mean in more than one way. Such a soul, wrote Giuseppe Prezzolini, belongs to an unregenerate mass with a troglodyte's mentality, barbarous in both mind and heart; the members of this mass live either isolated one from another or within the narrow circle of the family, a group "conceived in a rather beastly way."[40] The Italian people, Prezzolini elaborated, "are a herd" that should be led by shepherds, kings, or demagogues, and the worthlessness of the citizen is reflected in the soldier. Like the donkey, the soldier has an extraordinary "ability to suffer and to endure," but he is lazy and imprecise and has no love for his country, no discipline, and no sense of duty.[41] Even though Prezzolini recognized that the members of the "herd" had made many sacrifices and suffered a great deal during the war, he saw nothing good in them because he believed that they lacked character. "This [sacrifice and suffering] is not enough to make a people," Prezzolini wrote to Ardengo Soffici after the Italian defeat at Caporetto in 1917. "The people lack conscience and knowledge. There is everywhere little will, little belief, and little passion. There is no profound feeling of honor. There is no pride."[42] For his part, Ardengo Soffici believed that bestiality deprived the Italian soldier of manly endurance. In June 1917 the *vociano* artist, an infantry officer, was wounded and taken to a field hospital filled with soldiers who in civilian life were "laborers and peasants." He was prepared to witness some extraordinary manifestation of "animal primitivism" on the part of those soldiers; instead he noticed with surprise that they lay "totally unconscious," like stunned animals.[43]

A few writers who, unlike Papini and Prezzolini, had lived in the trenches and shared daily with the common soldier the hardship and danger of the front, saw the common man as the victim of a harsh destiny. They refrained from casting scorn and blame on him and from demanding his blood. They showed an understanding and compassion all too rare among intellectuals for the plight of the soldier-citizen. Piero Jahier knew that the *alpini* he led at the front were illiterates who as civilians lived wretchedly. He realized that their wretchedness might have induced them to join a revolution as a way to improve their lot, but never to make war for their country, because their country had done nothing for them. Their fatherland had given them not even an elementary education, no means of transportation to their place of work, no social or economic help. They lacked a political conscience; their country meant nothing to them. Jahier saw that his *alpini* submitted to war in the same way they had accepted the rigorous demands of their deprived civilian life, making adjustments to life at the front just as they had adjusted to the cruel drudgery of work at home. For them to make war was little different from eking out a miserable existence at home. Yet the *alpini* show a moving loyalty to their battalion because they know that it feeds and clothes them; to them the battalion "is the first fatherland they ever met." They love the officer who acts as a teacher and who shares with them the danger and stress of combat. In them grows a dedication to their duty stronger than the fear of death: "They would die . . . just to show that the *alpino* is not afraid." How rewarding for Italy and its military spirit, Jahier implies, had these men been given a reason to place their loyalty and dedication at the service of their country![44]

"An obscure sense of necessity" drives them, the *alpini* officer Paolo Monelli wrote of his men, and they accept it with resignation, because at home this same sense of necessity forces them to work for their own and their families' survival. For the *alpini*, war is only a variation on a losing struggle that lasts a lifetime.[45] These men have known only the desperation and exhaustion of brutal work, and they discharge their military duty with the same blind submission and desperation with which they strove for survival at home.[46] War would leave their fate unchanged. If death spared them, they would return, unknown and unrewarded, to their thankless toil, to face again their "harsh destiny."

Monelli, like Jahier, felt that the *alpini* placed their loyalty and their "serene and earnest courage" at the service of a country that did not deserve them.[47]

Instead of understanding and compassion for the common man, life in the trenches brought out contempt among those writers whose virulent patriotism and nationalism had led them to enlist. Carlo Emilio Gadda articulated with imagination the link between the fallen state of the Italian people and war. Gadda was commissioned second Lieutenant in the Alpine Corps in August 1915, fought in the Alps east of Trento, was captured, and spent the last year of the war in a prison camp near Hanover in Germany. After World War II he emerged as one of Italy's most distinguished writers. "For me and for my family," he wrote with patriotic fervor, "the Kingdom of Italy was a real, living thing, worthy of my service and support." He felt that war was necessary, and before joining up he demonstrated on the streets with the interventionists, shouting "long live D'Annunzio and death to Giolitti,"[48] prime minister from 1903 to 1914, and a staunch proponent of Italian neutrality.

Gadda's support of the war was fed by the same sense of guilt for the Italian past that tormented other intellectuals. Believing that Italians were egoists and cowards, Gadda was tormented by fear that he himself was tainted by those vices. He felt bitter and angry toward his countrymen, and he devoted many pages of his work to stigmatizing them. "This book," Gadda wrote in his *Giornale di guerra per l'anno 1916* (War diary of 1916), "vents the anger of a poor Italian soldier . . . full of bitterness for personal, family, patriotic, and ethnic reason."[49] Stirred by a fellow officer's refusal to obey an order from headquarters about cropping the hair, Gadda imparts to the irrelevant event a meaning that only demonstrates his hostile temper, bursting out: "To our stupid, swinish, doggish, bastard, boorish [Italian] soul [it] is a matter of personal dignity to say 'I do what I will, I have no master.'

This attitude is called pride, liberty, dignity." But, adds Gadda, in reality this attitude only shows the "idiotic egoism of the Italian who makes of everything a personal question, and who sees everywhere . . . egoism; this gives him the instinctive need to oppose to that egoism another poisonous, arbitrary egoism."[50]

Matters that touched Gadda himself evoked an even angrier response. The apparent loss of his officer file in the bureaucratic labyrinths, and the resulting delay in his advancement to first lieutenant enraged him to the point of calling the untidiness of Italians the mark of a "race of swine, of pigs, of beings capable only of disfiguring the world with disorder, and with the prolixity of their senseless acts." And at the front Gadda quickly detected the other vice of which Italians were accused: cowardice. For him, the soldiers dying at the front could not be called heroes because they lived and fought in the unrelenting grip of fear. These soldiers "are even afraid of the sound of rifle fire, they turn yellow at the mere sound of the enemy gun, and they wet their pants at the thought of far away danger . . . out of mere personal fear." Cebellini, Manerbi, and Mainetti, Gadda's comrades at the front, were gripped by what the writer calls "continual, ceaseless, consuming fear that makes [them] hide in the dugout like pregnant sluts."[51]

Gadda, in the eastern Alps in 1916, felt as Drieu La Rochelle did in August 1914 in the trenches of Charleroi, surrounded by cowardly comrades and needing to separate himself from that despicable mass. But whereas Drieu achieved his purpose through action, Gadda achieved his through words alone. He luxuriates in his noble feelings about military service and war, in marked contrast to the apathy and failure of his compatriots and comrades. "His" war, Gadda avers, was ruled by "a blind but true passion" and was "living discipline, the only one worth living for." He also remembers that when he was commissioned, "an intense quiver and a prideful pleasure benumbed" his "soul and freed him from all pain, remembrance, regret, and love." He wanted to be "a worthy Italian soldier," and let military duty and pride alone guide him. The idea of fighting for a better world, of fighting the war to end war, of fighting for a just cause had nothing to do with his support of the war or with his participation in it, Gadda confesses.[52] Gadda's submission to military duty had more to do with the precepts of Luigi Russo and Giovanni Boine about the value of military service and discipline as a cure for the individual and collective disease of the Italians.

Gadda's "blind passion" was occasionally interrupted by fits of "brutality, bestiality, rhetoric, and idiocy." Under fire, he "hugged the ground more than once," fatigue knocked him out, and sometimes he collapsed like "a worn-out horse." One frosty night in April 1916 on Mount Adamello he "let himself slip down on the icy ground like an exhausted mule" ready to die; at times he realized that the horror of the front brought him close to "madness." But his "military pride" saved his mind. Something else helped save Gadda—self-effacement. At the front, "to be, man had to disappear," and to survive, he had "not to be." If the soldier wanted to live like a man, he was doomed; but if he gave up his humanity, he might be able to survive. "The strong and the brave" that Gadda knew at the front were, as he says, soldiers who had willfully shed their humanity ("della loro umanità si disumanarono") .[53]

The reversion to a lower state leaves Gadda untroubled because the emotional environment of war gives him the "feeling of the sublime," and because he looks on the reversion as the appropriate sacrifice that will help cure Italy, and himself, of cowardice. In the *War Journal* Gadda looks back on his combat experience, when the mere noise of the battle gave him "a superhuman emotion" that multiplied his energy, his will, and his enthusiasm. He recalls "the divine" moments of danger, the "sublime" acts of battle; he cherishes them, the more so because they are gone forever, and in remembering, "an obsessing pain leading him to madness" overtakes him. He recognizes that as he was living those divine moments of danger, the torment of "the animal in danger" assailed him, but he alleges indifference to the torment because the desire to serve his fatherland, "to raise himself up" through action, and to ennoble somehow the "bag of rag into which fate was about to turn" him, drives him on. He is indifferent toward both victory and defeat because he values his fighting and suffering above all else, as the means to "the moral improvement" of his fatherland, and especially of himself. Gadda stresses his craving for redemption by portraying his decay through the words with which Beatrice in Purgatory chastised Dante's sinful life on earth: "This man in his early life was such potentially that every right disposition would have come to marvelous proof in him; but so much the more noxious and wild the ground becomes, with bad seed and untilled, as it has more good strength of soil."[54]

Gadda's pattern of thought—war as punishment for, and regeneration from, decay—runs through the pages of the Futurists, the Nationalists, and some *vociani*. The pattern recurs with a stridency and singlemindedness that set their writings apart from, and beneath, those of Croce and Russo. The Futurists and Nationalists prodded the people to make war, to face danger, to take risks, to suffer, and to die; they tried to cheapen the life of the common man, and to make him expendable. In the manifesto of the movement Marinetti founded, he proclaimed the "beauty and desirability of aggressiveness, danger, and war,"[55] for, in belligerency and combat, he saw the means to erase the vices that afflicted pre–World War I society. In *Guerra sola igiene del mondo* (War, the world's only hygiene), Marinetti conferred upon war the "hygienic" function of wiping out "indifference . . . unintelligent senility . . . and boorish pride."[56] The Futurist leader believed that for Italy—a kind of Third World country, "poor and prolific," with no possibility of improving the quality of life of its people—war and bloodshed were the only escape from economic and social misery: "For a poor and prolific nation war is good business." Besides, he argued, war would raise the moral level, for war had the power to call forth from everybody "courage, energy, and intelligence" in lightning-like manner.[57]

"The *dies irae* has come," wrote Giovanni Papini with relief in *Lacerba* when the war began. "A warm bath of black blood" was needed, and finally the people were getting it. "It is a wholesale slaughter," he continued gleefully. "Day after day man cuts throats, rips things up, disembowels, and tears things apart; he shatters and smashes things; he fires the rifle and the machine guns; he sets things on fire, and bombards them."[58] This frantic slaughter is good for the Italians, Papini wrote in agreement with Marinetti, because "we [Italians] are too many," because there is too much "rabble" and too many "idiots" among us, and because there is "an infinity of people who are absolutely useless and superfluous." War and slaughter would conveniently get rid of this worthless mass.[59]

Papini rationalized death in war by crudely rehashing Croce's idea that mankind has progressed, and will progress, only through bloodshed: "Without the sacrifice of many men mankind regresses; without a holocaust of human life, death would prevail upon us." Papini therefore urged the Italians: "We must fight . . . if we want civilization to progress." He insisted on Italian bloodshed because blood is the "oil needed by the wheels of the big machine [civilization] as it flies away from the past toward the future. . . . We need corpses to pave the road to triumph." Death powers the course of history: "The history of philosophy smells of burnt flesh; the history of religion lets out screams of dying men; the history of science smells of blood; the history of law echoes with the executioner's footstep." Because history for Papini has shown the perpetual need for murder and slaughter, the people should eagerly embrace war, where the opportunities to kill and to die abound; those who refuse to do so "are malefactors" and should be done away with.[60]

Papini failed to distinguish between wholesale, inescapable death on the battlefield and willful death for an ideal. He made no distinction because he wanted only to see the punishment of a people he believed to be worthless, whom he still branded as brutes after a year of war and sacrifice. In Papini's view, the Italians "are used to work from morning to night, from the first of January to the thirty-first of December; they ask only for a piece of bread and a slice of salami in daytime, a little lovemaking at night, and a glass of wine on Sunday." When these people are sent to the battlefield, they kill and are killed even though they do not know and "have never known why they fight."[61]

Papini was correct in accusing the Italian people of ignoring the cause for which they were going to fight and perhaps die. He was right also about their wretchedness. But in showing only contempt for that wretchedness, Papini ignored the responsiblilty for Italian misery, which lay with the ruling classes, who over the centuries had neglected and oppressed the common people. No one understood the drama of the Italian people and what was being done to them on the eve of the war better than Giuseppe Borgese:

> The peasants and workers, those in the field-grey uniform and those in the factories and on the farm . . . had behind them nearly twenty centuries of servitude and misery: from the Caesars, who had finally trodden down the spontaneity of the Mediterranean civilization under an Asiatic despotism, to the petty tyrants and users of their villages; from Nero . . . to the inquisitors and schoolmasters who had robbed all Southern peoples

> of Europe of any right to think and grow. They had learned obedience within the walls of their cold, evil-smelling homes, in those hives of family life whose honey was fear and worry; and in the churches . . . where the Kingdom of the Devil was often proclaimed under the name of the Kingdom of God, and Hell was promised to the sinner who did not like to serve and starve. . . . The people at large had faithfully obeyed for near two thousand years, happy when they were only allowed to kiss the hand of the lord, to hear the swishing silk gown of the lady, or just to cry in frenzy behind the wooden saint in procession that he might bestow an inch of rain on the shriveled crop of their acre. These people now . . . marched to the national and supernational war. . . . They just obeyed, as they always had. Obediently, they bled at the front; obediently they starved at home.[62]

A recent study of documents on public opinion compiled by the civil governors of the provinces shows that in April 1915 the Italian people "did not want war," that the peasants, the largest part of the lower class, "wanted peace," and that even the bourgeoisie, which included most of the interventionists, had "a very limited desire" to go to war to annex Trento, Trieste, and territories on the Adriatic coast.[63] The majority of the Italian people—poor, uneducated, with no political consciousness, their energy and time taken up by the difficult business of making a living—saw no reason why they should also bear the burden of the sacrifices that war would demand. Given the direction and strength of public opinion, it seemed inconceivable that within a month Italy would jump into the conflict.

Yet in early May 1915, ex–prime minister Giovanni Giolitti, who represented the party of neutrality and who still commanded the loyalty of three hundred deputies and over a hundred senators—the overwhelming parliamentary majority—sensed that the country was drifting toward war. Having underestimated the passion and drive of the hawkish minority, he could not believe that Italy was sliding into combat. He told the journalist Olindo Malagodi that the Italian "political leaders ought to be shot" if they allowed the interventionists to push Italy into the conflict. How can they drag the country into the war when the majority is against it, he asked in disbelief.[64]

Giolitti was shaken because he knew that, besides the opposition of the majority of Italians, another reason should have kept Italy neutral. Austria, prodded by Germany, was inching closer to yielding Trento, Trieste, and some territories on the Adriatic, the goals that Italy aimed to achieve by war. It was true that in April Italy had signed the Pact of London, which committed Italy to fight on the side of England and France, if it decided to enter the war. But the pact had no power to commit the country to war because the Italian parliament was never told about it. It was a tentative agreement and the stipulations of the pact were to become effective only if Italy joined the conflict by May 26.

Italy entered the war on May 24. "The small but aggressive interventionist party" prevailed over "the party of neutrality," large but lethargic, and over "the known will of the parliament."[65] As the parliament was for neutrality, pro-war Prime Minister Salandra presented his resignation to the king. Salandra's move stirred up the interventionists, who took things into their hands, descended into the piazzas of Italy, and demanded war. In Rome some of them stormed Montecitorio, broke windows, and insulted deputies. The king consulted with Giolitti, who refused to replace Salandra. Giolitti's refusal meant the abdication of neutralism. The deputies who supported neutrality felt betrayed by their leader, and many went along with Salandra, who resumed the premiership on May 16, his resignation having been turned down by King Vittorio Emanuele.[66]

Some historians look on May 16 as "the day when the constitution was abolished and liberty destroyed."[67] This view may be a bit pessimistic, but there is truth to it. In May "extra-parliamentary forces," taking advantage of the parliamentary crisis, managed to prevail over constitutional process. The arrogance and contempt that gave the intellectuals "the right and duty to interpret the destiny of their fellow citizens—the . . . humble ones, who would have to bear the burden and endure the sufferings of war," were finally transmuted into the intimidating fury of the interventionists. In what they, with a tragically warped sense of history, called "the radiant days of May," they "lashed Italy into war as one might whip a sleepy horse into a gallop."[68]

Nationalists, Futurists, and followers of both Gabriele D'Annunzio and Benito Mussolini, sharers of the ideas of men like Enrico Corradini and Giovanni Papini, played a key role in sending the Italian people to war.[69] On May 20, 1915 D'Annunzio harangued his followers in Rome, and before urging them to search for and beat up the deputies opposed to war he condemned neutrality and opposition to war as the signs of fear, cowardice, and deceit—the long-standing vices of the Italian people. He evoked a glorious battle of the Risorgimento on the Sesia River, where outnumbered and outgunned Italian troops fearlessly attacked and defeated the Austrians, and he proclaimed: "This courage, this impulse, this strength are the true virtues of our race." The rest he dismissed as nothing but corruption. D'Annunzio, for whom life was worthless unless lived dangerously, with death breathing down man's neck, urged: "Let us get rid of the corruptionists. War is the deliverer in all senses."[70] D'Annunzio spoke in the Roman Campidoglio, and the pealing of the bell on the capitol that accompanied the poet's words "seemed to call for war."[71]

Late in 1914 Mussolini became a supporter of the war, and he, too, likened neutrality to the vices of the Italians. In his newly founded daily newspaper, *Il popolo d'Italia*, he called opposition to war "cowardly propaganda" and asked: "Do we want to drag our miserable life on from day to day . . . or do we want to smash this dull and murky wall of intrigue and cowardice? Could not this be the time . . . to wake up the sleeping conscience of the populace and throw shovels of quicklime on the faces of the dead—and there are many in Italy—who foolishly regard themselves as living beings?"[72] Neutrality, the status quo, the preservation of jobs, peace of mind, even life itself, Mussolini insisted one month later in *Il popolo d'Italia*, are good only for "cowards, and Italy is full of them."[73] He looked on neutrality both as the living proof of Italian vices and as a cause of deepening degradation. What embitters, brutalizes, and kills one, he wrote early in 1915, "is indifference, shirking risk, irresponsibility, keeping 'neutral'; it is the attitude of the robber and of the hyena" that lurks and slinks while others fight. Magnifying the corruption of the Italians, Mussolini urged them to get rid of it by making war. Combat, he said, would finally "reveal Italy to the Italians," it would do away with the black legend of Italian pusillanimity, it would finally show the world that Italy can wage war, "a great war."[74]

One historian has recently shown that around 1914 Western European intellectuals called for war because they believed that it would redeem nations from decay.[75] The shrill condemnation of real and imaginary evils, and the fervid interventionism in the name of high-sounding ideals that swept Italy in the months and years before the outbreak of the hostilities, place Italy at the forefront of those European countries whose intellectuals advocated war in the name of redemption. But war redeemed no one. In the aftermath of the war no intellectual and no politician would claim that the Italian people were better off than in 1915. Even Benedetto Croce, that firm believer in the virtue of war, instead of rejoicing at the time of the armistice, looked on Italy as a convalescent coming out of a deadly disease, not as a reborn nation.[76] It was eventually realized that the war aim proclaimed by Prime Minister Salandra in 1915—"sacred egoism," that is, territorial gain—stripped the nation's immense sacrifice of its idealistic value[77] and made a mockery of the idea of redemption.

Some who thought they were fighting for redemption discovered that "war would regenerate neither Italy nor the Italians"[78] when the horrors of death on the battlefield confronted them. Others, keen observers of the military scene, exploded the hoax of redemption while the war was being fought. "War does not improve the people," in the words of an exceptionally thoughtful war diary written by Angelo Gatti, an aide to General Luigi Cadorna, the commander-in-chief of the Italian army. Mindful of the invectives and the incitements to war flung at the Italians, Gatti wrote in 1917 that it was useless to try to strengthen a weak man (Italy) while he is sick with acute pneumonia; first cure the pneumonia. War would do nothing for the Italian people, who suffered from a "growth crisis" and a lack of identity. Only a nation that has reached the peak of its strength, said Gatti, can afford to go to war; "to believe that a people can gain strength through war is both criminal and idiotic." Why then, Gatti asked, did Italy take to the battlefield? Because, he answered, in 1915 Italy was the victim of "idiots" and "criminals," the victim of "the D'Annunzios, of the Monicellis [Monicelli being a leading nationalist], of the *Idea nazionale* [the nationalist newspaper], of all the word-mongers of Italy."[79]

The idea of redemption by war was discredited also by

admirers of military bravery. War has no power to transform, wrote Lord Moran, a soldier on the Western Front and a student of the behavior of men under fire. War simply magnifies the good and the evil that exist in people, so that their virtues and vices become visible to everybody. War "cannot change, it exposes."[80]

Instead of bringing redemption, war dragged many combatants down, and not only on the battlefield. Four years after the victory at Vittorio Veneto, Italy, in becoming the prey of Mussolini's dictatorship, suffered a collective degradation. But war satisfied those intellectuals and politicians who looked on the people as decayed and worthless. War changed the contempt that Italian intellectuals and politicians felt for the people into contempt for their life. On the battlefield that contempt became the cult of the all-out offensive, the headquarters practice of sending the troops against enemy lines even though the chance of success was nil and death certain.

The doctrine of the so-called offensive *á outrance* was born in France at the turn of the century in the minds of General Foch and Colonel Louis de Grandmaison. At the Ećole Supérieure de la Guerre the doctrine was taught to the officers who were to lead the *poilus* against the German troops on the Western Front. The doctrine gained acceptance also outside France. The English used this tactic in 1917 in the swamps of Flanders at Passchendaele, where they lost a lot of men and made no territorial gain. The all-out offensive expressed English eagerness to fight, the patriotism of a nation in the "mood of self-sacrifice,"[81] the patriotism of a nation that "was straining every nerve to discharge an obligation of honor . . . France to be saved, Belgium righted, freedom and civilization re-won,"[82] and the patriotism of a soldier who wanted to show that he can be "the hero he has always wanted to be."[83]

France, unlike England and like Italy, used the offensive

á outrance as a means of atoning for national failings. The "insensate obstinacy and lack of comprehension" with which the French generals "continued to hurl the heroic but limited manhood of France at the strongest entrenchments, at uncut wire and innumerable machine guns served with cold skill"[84] was, as in Italy, rooted in the ground of national guilt and expiation. "War seems to us to be first a dreadful resignation, a renunciation, a humiliation . . . and you don't understand immediately the grandeur . . . of the asceticism it forces on us, of the *punishment* it lays on the fighting man," Henri Massis wrote from the trenches in January 1915.[85]

Ernest Psichari, whose military service in Africa just before the Great War had exalted him by revealing the very source of life,[86] passionately argued that defense on the battlefield was a dead strategy, befitting the generation born between 1855 and 1870. In the horrors of a German invasion, this generation was gripped by fear, possessed by "the soul of the loser," stripped of initiative, and able only to think and act defensively. But the generation to which Psichari belonged—that of 1914—had cast off the shadow of Sedan and repudiated the mentality of 1870, he believed. Psichari translated the new mentality into military spirit: "We men of the new generation have abandoned the ruinous theory of the defensive. We want to act, we want to impose our will on the enemy, we will attack him. The attack is the best defense."[87]

General Joffre condemned the defensive strategy as "a grave and profound evil" because it both "favoured the secret instinct of self-preservation" and undermined military discipline.[88] The spirit of the new generation, the *élan vital*, could achieve "great moral results," Henri Bergson said. True, the philosopher conceded, the price was high—"much blood and many tears." But, he believed, "an iron law" decrees that "material suffering" is the basis of human progress, and blood and tears should not stand in the way.[89]

Bergson's *élan vital* spilled over into military thought and practice, and became the soul of the offensive *á outrance.*[90]

From the beginning of the operations on the Austrian Front the Italian General Staff sent the infantry against the enemy lines in massed formation; for the Austrians, firing on the Italians "was easier than firing in the shooting gallery." If the infantrymen advanced close to the enemy lines they often encountered barbed wire that was intact despite artillery fire, and were mowed down by Austrian machine guns while they tried to cut the wire or to retreat to their trenches.[91] The offensive on Gorizia in the fall of 1915 left so many casualties that the attacking troops "walked over fields of corpses" from the units that had attacked before them.[92]

By November 1915 the Italian army had fought four of the twelve so-called Battles of the Isonzo, losing nearly a quarter of a million men, wounded or dead, along that river, but achieving no strategic or territorial gain.[93] It was "a crazy war," admitted General Enrico Caviglia,[94] and the madness of the first months set the trend of the war until the end of 1917. By October 1917 the army had fought "eleven battles of the Isonzo—and was still on the Isonzo,"[95] and the demoralized soldiers realized that they were in for "an organized slaughter."[96] Finally, "sickened" by "the limited results at unlimited cost" of the attrition strategy,[97] whose basic ingredient was the all-out offensive, the army in November 1917 yielded to the enemy at Caporetto. The Italians were forced west of the Isonzo to a new defensive line on the Piave River.

General Luigi Cadorna, who was reponsible for the conduct of the war on the Italian front, embraced the tactic of the offensive; even before the war he expounded its merits in a publication of the Army General Staff, *Attacco frontale e ammaestramento tattico* (Frontal attack and tactical training). The doctrine of the notorious booklet became the *vade mecum* of Cadorna and his generals up to the eleventh battle of the Isonzo. Mindless of the lethal results, Cadorna applied the doctrine of the offensive with unshakable faith, "wearing down the enemy by being worn down more than twice as fast."[98]

On the Western Front the votaries of the cult of the offensive ran into trouble with the politicians. After the costly failure of the offensive at Passchendaele in 1917, Prime Minister Lloyd George, who considered himself too weak to fire General Douglas Haig, restrained the enthusiasm of the commander in chief for the offensive strategy by keeping him so short of troops that the general could not even suggest a renewal of the British offensive.[99] Three French practitioners of the offensive *á outrance*—generals Joffre, Foch, and Nivelle—were dismissed in 1916 and 1917. But General Cadorna, though recognized as the most offensive-minded leader of the Great War, who always suffered more from attrition than his foe,[100] exhibited no restraint, held his post in spite of criticism and oppostion, and continued to apply the self-destructive doctrine of the offensive until late 1917, when the defeat at Caporetto made his dismissal imperative. Cardorna's extraordinary staying power in the face of huge losses of men and meager success against the enemy shows that the general enjoyed the support of the political leadership, which evidently had no qualms about his murderous strategy on the battlefield.

By the spring of 1917 the fiasco of the tenth battle of the Isonzo had convinced even the supporters and admirers of Cadorna that he had failed. Journalist Ugo Ojetti asked Colonel Gatti, "Why does Cadorna make war this way?" and commented: "Every battle he [Cadorna] starts ends in a disaster. . . . We cannot go on like this."[101] When Gatti realized that all the battles fought in 1917 "had ended badly," he asked himself: "How come has he [Cadorna] not grasped that there is something more important than tactic, something that has broken down, and that this something is man?"[102] Gatti understood that despite heavy losses of troops, Cadorna had not yet been defeated because the supply of men was abundant. Even the waste of men on a large scale apparently took nothing away from the strength of the Italian army because the dead and wounded were replaced by fresh troops. Cadorna cared about the judicious use of ammunition, and the number of shells and bullets available governed his battle plans. But the general had no concern for men. "I always heard him say: the lack of shells will end the battle; the battle will take this turn rather than that because we do not have enough shells; but I never heard him speak about the men and about using them economically." In the long run, Gatti concluded, the waste of soldiers will be fatal to Italy because its wealth of men, though great, will be exhausted.[103]

Cadorna took no reponsibility for the failure of the tenth battle of the Isonzo, placing the blame instead on the troops. Gatti recorded in his diary Cadorna's explanation "that the troops have not attacked as they ought to, that they had no faith, that they were indecisive, etc., etc."[104] This was no new complaint. On a similar occasion Cadorna had instituted what infantry Captain Luigi Gasparotto, an interventionist and a future minister of defense, styled "the discipline of terror,"[105] punishing what he thought to be lack of discipline and rebellion by "decimation." The French, too, used this method of punishment, but their military authorities could proceed with executions only if the president of the Republic approved. In contrast, General Cadorna's power of life and death over the troops was unrestrained by civilian authority until early 1917, when the government revoked that authority.

Cadorna was so eager to punish by execution that he extended the power to decree death to superior officers in the field, and made circumstantial evidence—not proof of guilt—sufficient grounds for execution. He prided himself on his discipline of terror and rewarded those who enforced it. On November 1, 1916, he learned that two days earlier eight soldiers had been executed "immediately and without trial" for acts of insubordination. Cadorna then sent a circular express letter to all army headquarters "to express ample and unconditional praise" for General Cigliana, the army corps commander responsible for ordering the executions, and to hold him up as a model.[106]

The discipline of terror gratified Cadorna, who thought it yielded excellent results. In June 1917, for instance, two regiments of the thirty-third division "attacked only because execution by shooting was in force."[107] In January 1917, when Malagodi described the army as being in a state of "impressing" demoralization, Cadorna admitted that after almost two years of war the soldiers were tired, but he also made it clear that the cure for weariness was death—not rest or better treatment. "Discipline is good now," he told Malagodi, "but for a while there have been hints of rebellion and some mutinies. The country was undisciplined, and so was the army; we have taken care of the problems by the usual and proper means, the shooting of the insubordinates to prevent the sparks from turning into a fire."[108] Summary trials and executions were an extension of Cadorna's cult of the offensive. The general had spun out a spiral of violence: "His way of making war amounted to a sentence of death for the soldiers; then, the only way to send them over the top was to threaten them with a death more certain and more ignominious, if they refused to attack."[109]

Why the cult of the offensive and the discipline of terror? The words General Cadorna spoke to Malagodi early in 1917 ("the country was undisciplined, and so was the army") show that the general's policy was governed partly by his view of the men he led on the battlefield, not by military criteria alone. Italy in 1915, he wrote in *La guerra sulla fronte italiana*

(War on the Italian front), "was morally unprepared for the war."[110] The discipline in the army was poor because the Italian people were "antimilitarist." The men came into the army against their will and, infected by propaganda "against our institutions," carried out their duties only because they feared punishment, sang songs inspired by the desire to leave the army, and then went home unchanged by military education.[111] For Cadorna, the truth was that in 1915 the Italians had no "social" or "interior" discipline and no "sense of duty" to raise themselves "to great moral heights." "Social" and "interior" indiscipline was an "old evil" of the Italian race, Cadorna thought. It could be traced back to the age of the Communes, when citizens of the same town fought one against another, and to the Renaissance, when individualism ruled and Torquato Tasso realized that the Italians had many virtues but not "discipline." Cadorna even praised Germany, the old enemy, because he believed that its "profound" social discipline enabled it to fight on for four years and prove to the world the moral superiority of the German people (he ignored the fact that after fighting for four years Germany lost the war).[112]

Believing that the discipline of the army reflected the discipline of the people, Cadorna transmuted the "interior indiscipline" of the Italian people from a kind of national degeneration into the first cause of the Italian defeat at Caporetto.[113] Directly after that defeat the general rejected responsibility for the collapse of the Italian army and the Austrian breakthrough, telling colonel Gatti: "What could I do; the army was swarming with worms."[114] To Malagodi the general made it clear that the cause of the debacle was the indiscipline and cowardice of the troops: "It was not even a battle turned into panic; it was a rebellion . . . a defection, a military strike without historical precedent. More than half a million men suddenly refused to fight; they believed they could end the war by throwing their weapons away and by going home."[115] In that moment of truth, when the Italian people finally said no to the abuses of the elite, they were branded once more as worthless and charged with the responsibility for the military failure. After Caporetto Ugo Ojetti, the art critic in uniform who never fought yet garnered medals, wrote: "We are a people of lazybones, of crooks, of irresponsible persons, of servants. Only a minority is made up of real men. Our independence is only a political abstraction because it has no moral substance and no continuity of purposes and deeds. . . . Out of forty million people . . . thirty-nine are 'drifters'—and there is no remedy."[116]

Caporetto gave Cadorna a threefold opportunity: to absolve himself from his failure as a general, to pin the failure on the Italian soldier, and to justify the discipline of terror he had instituted. In his memoirs, the general recalled that as early as May 1915 he had ordered the enforcement of "an iron discipline" throughout the army, although such discipline ought to come "from the bottom of the soul" because "spiritual and formal discipline, are inseparable." Unfortunately, the Italian people had neither spiritual nor formal discipline, and "it is impossible to find in the army interior discipline if the nation has none." Cadorna concluded: "When there is no interior discipline, then exterior discipline is needed." Even though applied in its severest form, the general argued, the "exterior discipline" (and one can easily imagine what that neutral term covered) cannot prevent military disasters such as that of Caporetto.[117] In any case, the discipline of terror continued to appeal to Cadorna, and in the days after the rout of Caporetto disoriented troops and officers, swallowed in the chaotic retreat, were randomly picked up by the military police at strategic crossings and summarily executed.[118]

Although Army Commander Luigi Capello had some disagreements with General Cadorna on battle plans and tactics, the two agreed on the baseness of the Italian people and on the need to shape them up by discipline and bloodshed. General Capello applied to the troops his own brand of discipline of terror, and earned fame as "the bloodthirsty one" and "the butcher" by wasting them in hopeless attacks on the Isonzo front.[119] He felt constrained to explain his harsh treatment of the troops, and he dug, as did many intellectuals before and during the war, into the supposed vices of the Italian people: before the war the national conscience was fickle, skeptical, and meddlesome; "personal interest" ruled it, and as a result the Italians lacked a sense of duty, opposed military service, and abhorred war. Lofty ideas about "the rights of man" and "humanitarian theories" worsened the irresponsibility of the Italians and made them hope, foolishly, to be able to stop the "irresistible motion" of "the wheels of war."[120] That illusion was perhaps one facet of the nation's false "optimism," the blindness of the ostrich that fights danger by hiding its head in the sand; the improvidence of the *lazzarone* who spends all the money he has for breakfast and then lies idle all day, oblivious of the future; the self-deceit that masked the nation's inertia and its inability to face reality.[121]

The temper of the Italian people had still to be forged, General Capello believed, and for him the way to do it was to throw Italians into demanding and dangerous battles. "An intimate and profound conviction," the general confided, "leads me to place very great value on the invigorating function of the offensive."[122] That conviction came from what Capello styled his "profound knowledge of the psyche of our people," which looked on the attacker as the strong and the defender as weak;[123] for the Italian soldier to feel strong and fearless, he had to attack, not wait for the enemy to rush at him. Other reasons dictated Capello's preference for the offensive. The abundance of troops (thirty six Italian versus twenty Austrian divisions in the field at the start of the conflict) led Capello, like Cadorna, to use men recklessly and to disregard the heavy losses that the all-out offensive produced. Capello admitted that the army was well supplied with men but poorly supplied with arms[124] (in the spring of 1915 hand grenades were unknown, and some officers went into the first actions of the war having no side arms),[125] but he never mentioned the glut of men as the reason for the persistent use of the offensive strategy. He explained the role of manpower in battle in terms of both the moral sickness of the people and the therapeutic value of war and bloodshed.

True, Capello wrote, the soldier fights "with rifle, gun, and heavy mortar"; but "he only wins with his soul."[126] Those who emphasize the role of the mortar in the battle for Gorizia in August 1916, Capello pointed out, forget that the victory was gained by "the Italian soul," not by the mortar; "our people . . . must know that victory goes to the soldier who handles the weapon, not to the steel instrument." He belittled the spirit of the French and the English on the Western Front: "They have many more guns and mortars than we have, yet in two months of offensive on the Somme in the summer the allies gained less than we did in only three days on our front." And he praised his soldiers: "You should have seen our soldiers when they went over the top," the general wrote excitedly about his troops attacking Gorizia; they "threw themselves forward . . . in a compact mass, impetuous, confident . . . and ready to overcome the enemy." To the general, the success of the attack was "the work of the heart, mind, faith, enthusiasm, and reason." Having discovered the uselessness of weapons and the primacy of human qualities, the general assigned to the victory at Gorizia "a moral value." He held up the intangible qualities forged in the heat of the battle as the traits that the Italians needed to better themselves as a people: "This, Italy needs! Steely souls able to carry the burden of present and future struggles."[127]

Did General Capello play up the virtue of the offensive

and the strength forged in battle as the means to build up the moral tone of the Italian soldiers and make them better citizens, or to justify throwing away their lives? It is hard to believe that a general who in the course of the war earned the reputation of "butcher" would be concerned about the ethical improvement of the men under his command. Another combatant who praised the virtue of the offensive was only a corporal in the Great War, but in a few years would wield so much power that, under the pretense of regenerating the Italian people by way of Fascism, he would set out to destroy by war the very people he professed to lead to salvation. "A hundred thousand guns," Benito Mussolini wrote from the front in 1916, "will not give us victory. Italy will win only if the soldier will move out to the offensive and if he will show the courage to come out of his defensive positions and to face death."[128]

Capello's reflections about the uplifting effect of the offensive on the soldier's morale might sound somewhat convincing if the circumstances of the attack on Gorizia were ignored. The attack succeeded and casualties were only moderate because, luckily for the Italians, the Austrians were slow to bring their machine guns out of their rocky dugouts and to open fire on the advancing infantrymen when the Italian artillery lifted the preparatory barrage. Had the Austrians acted quickly, Capello himself recognized, "they would have slaughtered our soldiers."[129] Italian headquarters launched many offensives on the Isonzo front, but none of them succeeded as well, and none of them cost as little in troops, as the attack on Gorizia. Yet could any of the protagonists feel, as General Capello wrote they did, that facing the enemy's guns worked up their "heart, mind, faith, enthusiasm, and reason"?

Emilio Lussu's *Un anno sull'altipiano* describes the assault of one battalion of the Sassari brigade on the Austrian trenches of the Asiago Plateau. In the summer of 1916 these trenches, dug out of the rocky terrain and defended by machine guns, had been attacked several times by the same brigade, without success and with many casualties. Both the troops and headquarters had realized that the Austrian position was impregnable. Nevertheless, in July headquarters ordered a new attack. "The assault! Where are we going?" asked Lussu hopelessly as he got ready to lead his company over the top. "We leave cover and go out in the open. Where? Every machine gun, crouched on its cartridge-filled belly, waited for us. He who has not known this moment has not known war." It was "the most terrible" instant.[130] The men knew that they had no chance of victory and that the attack would kill them. But they advanced into the open ground of a valley; when the Austrian machine guns opened up and started cutting the Italians down, the survivors kept advancing and falling; out of a thousand men "only a few" came close to the Austrian trenches, Lussu among them. He could see now that the defenders stood erect outside their dugouts. "They felt safe. Many even stood on the parapets. All aimed calmly and fired at us as if they were on the parade ground." Then something extraordinary happened: "Suddenly the Austrians stopped shooting. Those in front of me had wide-open eyes and an expression of terror on their faces, almost as if they, not us, were under fire. One of them . . . shouted in Italian 'Stop! Stop!' and others on the trench parapet repeated the same words. The first Austrian again . . . said: 'Stop, brave soldiers. Don't make us kill you!'"[131] The enemy, feeling both pity and terror for the Italian troops, refused to bring about what Italian headquarters had willed—the destruction of its own soldiers.

The contempt of headquarters for the life of the soldier, the heart of Lussu's narration, is shown also on the fringes of the hopeless attack. General Leone, the divisional commander who ordered the attack but stayed in the trenches while his advancing troops were slaughtered, knew that the attack was doomed and that the troops were being killed needlessly. He watched impassively from the safety of the dugout "like an inquisitor determined to watch over the execution of the condemned to the very end." After the desperate action, the surviving officers felt the threat of madness, born of the realization that they had been condemned to death without reason. "I am afraid I am going crazy," one of them told Lussu. "I will go crazy. One of these days I will kill myself. One has to kill oneself." Lussu, too, "felt waves of madness approaching and receding." Sometimes, he confessed, "I felt my brain flapping inside my skull like water in a shaken jar."[132] The murderousness of headquarters' orders in this latest action led the surviving soldiers to fear their generals as much as, or more than, their enemy. Lieutenant Ottolenghi of Lussu's battalion, the protagonist of several suicidal attacks, would conclude that "our generals seem to have been sent by the enemy to destroy us."[133]

One reason why headquarters' orders became slaughter on the battlefield was that the superior officers at the front acquiesced in headquarters' plans, no matter how difficult or unreasonable. These officers acted out of fear of disciplinary measures or for the sake of their careers. Just before the offensive on the Bainsizza Plateau in June 1917, Colonel Gatti visited the front and noticed "everywhere . . . a sense of void."[134] He spoke about his finding to Colonel Roberto Bencivenga, the best military mind and the hardest worker on the general staff. Bencivenga knew a few of the defects in the operations on the Bainsizza. One of them, he told Gatti, was that the field commanders "had taken on the habit of judging everything as easy to do and, to keep their position, of displaying a faith in the planned operations which they really did not have." Taught by experience that he who points out difficulties loses his job, the commanders faked ease of execution and confidence in success. "Can this action succeed?" the general staff would ask. "Sure!" the commanders replied. "Is it easy or hard?" "Oh, easy."[135]

Paolo Monelli wrote of a major in the Alpine Corps on the Asiago Plateau who received the order to send his men into an action he knew was hopeless. He agreed to "the stupid order of death . . . with an even, idiotic smile" because he calculated that if his "battalion let itself be properly slaughtered," he would then get a promotion.[136] Headquarters' requests troubled the conscience of some officers in the field, who showed more concern about the safety of their men than about pleasing headquarters. One general issued an order of the day promising his troops and officers that he would refrain from sending them against the extremely well fortified Austrian positions on Mount Podgora.[137]

Carlo Salsa's war experience reveals that even early in the war the general staff was disregarding the enemy's strength and sending troops to their death in futile offensives. The officers' contempt for the men went as far as taunting those who submitted to the slaughter with reluctance. In November 1915 Salsa, the author of *Trincee* (Trenches), led his men up the slopes of Mount San Michele to relieve a company of infantrymen. The lieutenant in charge, a veteran of the Isonzo front, told Salsa the fate of the regiments sent to fight there that summer:

> They were hurled against this barrier called Carso [a rocky plateau east of Gorizia]. Waves of young, enthusiastic, unknowing, and generous soldiers rushed this wall of stones and mud. . . . We came up against the first trenches protected by barbed wire. The barbed wire! Courage can do nothing against this miserable and terrible thing. We had no tools to cut it, and the human waves caught in these iron cobwebs broke as if they had hit a rocky cliff. . . . On Mount San Michele,

> at San Martino, on Mount Sei Busi, on the Doberdò Plateau, and along the Selz ridges the human tide was blindly flung up the slopes of the deadly quarry against the fierce enemy defenses: human flesh against brute matter, springtime energy against the waiting machine, valor against the concealed trap; and everywhere the rallying cry of the attackers was muted by the cold stammering of the machine gun. . . . The ground was strewn with corpses; all the regiments were nearly wiped out: without artillery support, without mortar, without anything, it was impossible to move forward.[138]

At this point the narrator, at a loss to explain why the troops were senselessly sacrificed, simply reports that "headquarters had gone crazy." They issued crazy orders that admitted of no discussion and no delay in execution: "Forward! We can't! What does it matter? Forward just the same. But the barbed wire is uncut! What a reason! Cut the barbed wire with your chests, with your teeth, or with your trowels. Forward! It was drunkenness." Imbued with the idea that success depended more on "heart, mind, faith, enthusiasm, and reason" than on weapons and equipment, headquarters held the soldiers responsible for the failure to conquer, ascribing it to their truancy and cowardice. The hopeless attacks ordered against the enemy trenches became the punishment for the supposed cowardice and failure of the troops. Headquarters set in motion a vicious cycle. Each slaughter and failure became an excuse for sending more troops into action fated to end, again, in death and failure. The generals made good the losses that each action caused as best they could, "and then they said, 'Let us go, you truant infantrymen, to the assault.' " The infantry was ordered to rush intact defenses even in broad daylight, and when the troops went over the top and onto open ground, death reaped them: "The Austrians were delighted: to make sure that nobody got away alive, they let us go all the way to the barbed wire without firing a shot, and then they started the music."[139]

The unrelenting offensives and the mounting casualties told the soldier he could expect nothing but death or wounds at the front, and he resigned himself to his fate. The narrator in Salsa's novel remembers that at the very beginning of the war, when slaughter was still unknown to the soldiers, they took big risks, and many of them volunteered to crawl close to the enemy's trenches at night to place dynamite beneath the barbed wire. But now, they act like "an inert, disheartened herd" and take mortal risks only because they know they are doomed anyway. They say, "It is my turn," and they go to their death "like donkeys driven to the chopping block by cudgel strokes."[140] When Salsa saw soldiers at the front treated like animals, he was unable to understand the reason. He wrote his novel-memoir right after the war, at a point when he lacked the historical perspective to realize that the soldiers were abused like beasts because they were regarded as beasts. Salsa could not see that the soldiers had arrived at the front bearing the stigma of degradation placed on them by intellectuals and politicians, and that on the battlefield degradation legitimized annihilation.

In their memoirs both General Cadorna and General Capello, we saw, justified the self-destructive strategies they used on the battlefield by the fulfillment of civic and ethical ideals. The offenses "were bloody but useful," in the words of Senator Luigi Albertini, the editor of the *Corriere della sera* during the war years, who had firsthand knowledge of the front, who knew of the methods of attack used there, and who supported them. In his war memoirs he wrote that the attacks gave the troops and the officers "experience, maturity, tradition, and glory."[141] He also thought that the national reputation was proportionate to the losses in the battlefield; a lesser "contribution of blood" by Italy, he feared, would have shamed the nation.[142] And a historian has written that the six hundred thousand men who died in the war erased the reputation for cowardice that for centuries had burdened the Italian people.[143] But the soldiers in the field knew better than their leaders and their historians why their lives were being wasted. Like the infantryman in Lussu's battalion who bet against a respite from offensive actions, the soldiers knew that they were regarded as inferior beings and their life as worthless. To the comrade who bet that after three consecutive assaults on the Austrian positions, the troops would be spared another bloodbath the next day, the infantryman replied: "And why should there not be one more [assault]? Are we not sons of a bitch?" The next day the battalion went over the top, and eight hundred men out of a thousand were wiped out.[144]

Although the common soldier knew that he was regarded as worthless and that he was doomed, he was unable to grasp the root of his problem—the responsibility of the leadership—and thus could articulate no response to it. The dilemma was articulated instead by the officers, better educated than the troops. Toward the end of Emilio Lussu's *Un anno sull'altipiano*, an unusual conversation occurs among the officers of Lussu's regiment. This regiment, deprived of its rest period after fighting on the Asiago Plateau in mid-1917, had rebelled, but the officers had checked the mutiny by peaceful means. Lussu takes great pain to identify the speakers by name and to report the words they spoke immediately after the mutiny was quelled. He attaches great importance to what the officers had to say, especially to the words of Lieutenant Ottolenghi, who shows what the common soldiers were unable to see: the responsibility of the political and military leadership in causing their misery and destruction. Ottolenghi regrets that the mutiny failed, blaming the outcome on the mistake of revolting, unarmed, in nighttime. But he also defends the mutinous soldiers as having "a thousand reasons" to mutiny, and says he would join them should they attempt another revolt. Accusing him of disloyalty and treachery, some of his fellow officers point out to him that if other troops and officers followed his lead, the enemy would win without fighting. The lieutenant replies that for the Italian soldiers and the subordinate officers, the enemy's victory would be no worse than the "miserable slaughter" now taking place on the battlefield. In any case, Lieutenant Ottolonghi adds, the Italian people as a whole would not suffer if the enemy won, because the wickedness of the Austrian leaders only equals that of their Italian counterparts. If the Italian people were willing to spill their blood, they should create a revolution, which might buy freedom from economic and political servitude, rather than making war, which for them means "useless carnage" brought about by the leadership for the sake of slaughter. Our political and military leaders, Ottolenghi declares, "seem to have been sent us . . . to destroy us." The solution is an about-face in which mutinous units start firing on their superior officers, because the enemy of the Italian soldier lies not across no-man's-land, but at his back. "I would start" the shooting, Ottolenghi proposes, "with the commander of the division, whoever he is," and then "I would work my way up the hierarchy, methodically and relentlessly . . . all the way up to Rome. There the great enemy headquarters stands."[145]

The bloodbath that the Italian leadership had envisioned as the path to national renewal and glory was now spawning only despair and hatred.

3. A Loss beyond Life

Even after Italy had been at war for more than a year, and its army had been bleeding and dying in futile attempts to break through the Austrian defenses, Benedetto Croce extolled with philosophical imperturbability the nobility of war and death. Only national crisis, only war, he wrote in August 1916, brings to the fore the good men, the men who act and who love without making a show, the men who stand apart from the rabble, full of vices and deceit. "War, and even more Death, bring [the good men] out of the shadow and into the open, make known the course of their lives to the rest of us, and sometimes allow us to read the grave and moving words they have written."[1] This reflection drew inspiration from the death at the front of a southern Italian officer, Emilio Ricci, whose life and poems are now all but forgotten despite Croce's tribute to him. Penned in the Neapolitan philosopher's ivory tower, a thousand miles from the battlefield, Croce's reflection must have sounded hollow to a soldier at the front, facing death himself.

The historian Adolfo Omodeo was of the same southern intellectual elite as Croce, wanting to help create "the new fatherland" and a "new Italian conscience." Leaving his scholar's study, Omodeo enlisted as a lieutenant in June 1915, one month after Italy entered the European war. At the front, he quickly learned that death generates neither exalted feeling nor high-flown rhetoric. He learned that even the threat of death that hung over the soldiers daily killed idealistic motives and enthusiasm for war. "Very rarely do I say the word 'fatherland' in front of my men," Omodeo wrote to his wife; "I never use big words: faced with the real vision of death, my men are suspicious and unresponsive to enthusiasm; and enthusiasm, believe me, has to be well rooted and has to be supported by faith to survive here."[2]

The "realistic" vision of death dampened enthusiasm, even that rooted in the conviction that the cause of war was just. The physical environment of the battlefield, for instance, humiliated the combatant, and eroded any worth or nobility he might find in the death awaiting him. "This hill where we have come to die," Giani Stuparich wrote of the Italian positions around Monfalcone, "becomes barren and turns slowly into a dungheap," a mean place to sacrifice one's life. "Everywhere we tread on excrement that stinks unbearably. There are no latrines and everyone evacuates in the open and as close as possible to the dugout; the haste and the fear of being hit eliminate all decency." An *irredento*, Stuparich had fled Austrian-occupied territory to fight on the Italian side against the abhorred enemy. But neither hatred for the enemy nor love for his fatherland reinforced his courage or his endurance when he came face to face with death. He found support only in the instinct of self-preservation. Under a barrage of gunfire Stuparich cowers beneath a rock and sets his will to live against hovering death: "I strain with all my strength against death: I have the impression that one moment alone of neglect or relaxation will bring me death."[3]

Patriotism might induce the civilian to become a soldier, but it gave him little courage on the battlefield; the threat of death instead stirred the survival instinct. After four days and four nights in the snow-covered open country overlooking St. Quentin on the Somme, the poet Wilfred Owen wrote to his mother in the spring of 1917 that he was staying alive on brandy and on "the fear of death."[4]

Some military and civilian circles viewed death on the battlefield as glorious, as the proper end to fighting. On the battlefield itself, the frequency and visibility of casualties ironically bore out the idea that death, not survival, was the common lot of the soldier. But the men in the field rebelled in spirit against the concept of the ineluctability of death. When Carlo Salsa and other junior officers joined their infantry brigade at the foot of the San Michele mountain on the Italian-Austrian front late in 1915, the commanding general reminded them by way of greeting that they were replacing officers who had "died heroically," and urged the newcomers to make themselves worthy of their fallen predecessors. Salsa and his fellow officers made no reply but inwardly sneered at the general, who they thought was giving his "condolences" in advance, as though he considered them already dead.[5] "It is beautiful to die for one's country," solemnly intoned the lord mayor of Aiello in front of the soldiers of Emilio Lussu's brigade who, after their first tour of duty in the trenches, had returned to the village for rest. "Nobody liked his [the mayor's] hint, not even the colonel," Lussu deduced from the mute response of the listeners. "The sentence was classic, but the mayor was not the man to make us appreciate . . . the beauty of a glorious death. . . . He seemed to tell us: 'You are more handsome as corpses than as living men.' The officers coughed and threw a contemptuous look at the mayor."[6]

In May 1916 General Cadorna, the commander in chief of the Italian army, inspected Attilio Frescura's division on the Asiago Plateau and, knowing that the front was thin there, he called for all the soldiers of the division to hold the line no matter what. "I drink," he said at the dinner table there, "to the health of the beautiful division whose soldiers will all die rather than yielding one inch of ground." How the general could reconcile "our health with death" Frescura failed to see.[7] Siegfried Sassoon used irony to represent the fate that the death-prone mentality thrust upon the soldier:

> "Good-morning: good-morning!" the General said
> When we met him last week on our way to the line,

Now the soldiers he smiled at are most of 'em dead,
And we are cursing his staff for incompetent swine.
"He's a cheery old card," grunted Harry to Jack
As they slogged up to Arras with rifle and pack.
. . . .
But he did for them both by his plan of attack.[8]

The irony of the poem lies in the general's jauntiness, which at first glance suggests vitality and confidence in life. But the general means something quite different; his unspoken words to the troops are: "I am sending you to your death, and I don't care." Because these soldiers are cheated of a chance to voice their opposition, "the General" of the poem appears more subtle than either Salsa's or Lussu's representation of military and civilian authority, whose call for death is met by the intended victims' hostile response.[9]

In the spring of 1915, as if the game of "The General" had been discovered, the second battalion of the Welsh Regiment sang a song that said no to death:

I want to go home,
I want to go home.
The coal-box and shrapnel they whistle and roar,
I don't want to go to the trenches no more.
. . . .
Oh, I
Don't want to die,
I want to go home.

Around Christmas time of the same year Englishmen began hearing this same song at Victoria Station in London, where the troops were leaving for France.[10]

Louis-Ferdinand Céline, who was wounded in October 1914 near Ypres and cited for heroic conduct under fire, creates in the fictional *Journey to the End of the Night* a protagonist the opposite of himself. Bardamu opposes death at all costs. On leave from the front, he sits down with his friend Lola at a café in Paris, where he is seized by the fear that the lounging crowd is about to be shot. "Run, all of you," he shouts at the people sitting around him. "Get out! They're going to fire! They'll kill you. They'll kill us all." Dragged away to his friend's hotel, Bardamu again imagines that "all the people are going to get themselves shot." The fear of death and dying that Bardamu has brought back from the front is intensified by Lola who, Bardamu says, insists on praising "the death which was confronting us [soldiers], persistently, obscenely." Hospital care calms him down, but does not cure him. "Fear can't be cured," he explains. He says he will not allow the cremation of his body, because a dead body still retains the appearance of life, and even in death Bardamu wants to keep the illusion of life by preserving the body. When Lola repudiates him as a coward, he is unruffled because he loves life too well: "I refuse to accept war and all that it entails . . . because I am the only one who knows what I want. I want not to die." As a soldier, he saw himself a "man condemned to death"; as a man, he rebels against his fate and against Lola, who cannot see that, although he is doomed, he "might still not want to die."[11]

The protests of the soldiers imaginatively portrayed by Salsa, Lussu, Sassoon, and Céline were a fragile defense against the military cast of mind that held life cheap and death dear. "The supreme duty of the soldier is to fight and not to die," wrote General J.F.C. Fuller, thinking of the excessive number of lives wasted in the Great War. The tragedy was that "the military monks . . . were so immersed in the scholasticism of dead wars that they forgot that the soldiers . . . were living beings dreading death, yet willing to face battle as long as facing it did not mean willful suicide."[12] But the strategy of the military "monks"—"unlimited offensive"—called indeed for willful suicide, and the soldiers who faced battle were the victims of "unlimited slaughter."[13]

During 1915 the French, with British help, "hurled themselves again and again on the entrenched front in the west. Each time Joffre . . . found that the defenses had grown stronger in the interval. At the end of the year he had blunted the sword of France, so immense were his losses in this vain sacrifice."[14] Despite the knowledge that the ground around Loos in Artois was "bare and open . . . and so swept by rifle and machine-gun fire" from the German trenches and the numerous fortified villages immediately behind them that it would be folly to attempt to take the town, the English, led by Sir John French, launched an offensive in September of 1915.

Among the attacking 47th, 15th, and 9th divisions "casualties were heavy" and "varied from mere decimation to whole battalions being virtually obliterated." Two more divisions, the 24th and 21st, attacked on the second day of the action, and as the 24th came within range of the enemy's rifles and machine guns, it offered "such a target as had never been seen before." When the Germans began firing, the British troops "could be seen falling literally in hundreds." And when the 21st Division attacked, "whole battalions were annihilated"; the slaughter was so "revolting and nauseating" that the Germans out of pity stopped firing when the English began retreating.[15] As late as 1917 the French infantry was still being wasted on a large scale. General Nivelle's sinister notoriety grew out of his attempt to break through the shortened, formidable "Hindenburg Line." The offensive was met by "a disastrous repulse" that led to widespread mutinies among the French troops, "sick of being thrown against unsubdued machine guns."[16]

Unlimited offensives at extreme human cost caused mutinies among the Italian troops as well, especially in 1917 when they had fought most of the "Twelve Battles of the Isonzo," incurring large losses and making no gains. These rebellions were suppressed at the cost of more lives. Suicidal offensives nurtured a state of mind far more widespread than open rebelliousness, namely, resignation to death. A military historian has likened this apathy to the passivity of inmates facing extermination in Nazi death camps. On July 1, 1916, the first day of the offensive on the Somme—which on this day alone killed twenty thousand dead to no avail—the British trenches "were the concentration camps of the First World War," where soldiers waited their turn to die. "There is something Treblinka-like about almost all accounts of July 1st, about those long docile lines of young men, shoddily uniformed, heavily burdened . . . plodding forward across a featureless landscape to their own extermination inside the barbed wire."[17]

The mass killing beyond comprehension may have terrorized the soldier, but his sense of powerlessness brought out in him indifference and resignation. In the fall of 1915 a soldier in Robert Graves's company, while waiting on the fire-step for the order to go over the top at Loos, saw that the German machine guns, left intact by the preceding bombardment, were cutting down the advancing British troops. In terror he turned to Graves: "It's murder, Sir." The leader replied: "Of course, it's murder, you bloody fool. . . . And there's nothing else for it, is there?"[18] The French soldier, too, "has learned . . . to die at any moment, because he no longer thinks of the risks he runs at the front," Adrien Bertrand noted after almost two years of war. "Such has become [his] resignation and . . . his acceptance to live side by side with death."[19]

In the same battle that Robert Graves watched but had the good luck to avoid, the sacrifice of the two divisions of the 11th Corps suggested to Alan Clark that the troops resigned themselves to death because they believed in England as a civilization, so they submitted to an untimely death out of patriotism: "These men were volunteers. They were the flower of the richest, most powerful nation on earth. Behind them stretched the ordered childhoods of Victorian Britain; decency, regularity, a Christian upbringing; a concept of chivalry; overriding faith in the inevitable triumph of right over wrong; such notions were imbued in them. This had been their first time in action but if these were the rules of the game, well then, they would conform."[20]

But on the Italian front, where only a handful of volunteers fought, while most of the combatants were conscripts, the troops knew no patriotic or political ideals. They went to their death with the mindless resignation of cattle driven to the slaughterhouse, or like the victims of an unjust but irrevocable death sentence. The infantry "attacks to get out of the trenches . . . because it must obey and because there is nothing else to do," Curzio Malaparte, novelist and combatant, recalls about the scenes he witnessed. "The infantry advances. Slow, inexorable, listless, but not quite like a herd. The herd moves but does not understand; the infantrymen understand but they do not want to know. What does it matter to know why one must die? . . . It is our turn: we are fated." And so, "without a protest," the infantrymen went "to stretch their corpses" on the enemy's barbed wire "like rags on the clothesline."[21] Sometimes the soldier saw himself as the plaything of a cruel executioner. "We," Paolo Monelli wrote of himself and of the *alpini* he led, "have been put in a bag, and from time to time the cheerful butcher opens it, and throws us on the bloody bench. When it [the battle] is finished, the butcher picks up those of us still able [to face another battle], and puts us back into his bag."[22]

In June 1917, when demoralization among the troops approached critical proportions that would become tangible in the defeat of Caporetto, senior officers on the battlefield reported that around Monfalcone and on Mount Santo the troops, knowing the uselessness of their effort, wept as they attacked. "They did not rebel: when they were pushed out of their trenches, they went [toward the enemy]; but they cried."[23] Even the patriot sometimes succumbed to resignation; after his unit repeatedly but unsuccessfully attacked the Austrian trenches near Monfalcone, Giani Stuparich wrote: "I think . . . I will have to die. . . . We have realized that in war, one dies first; then one fights, then one wins or loses; lastly, there is the faint hope that one will survive, wounded or unhurt."[24]

When superior officers tried to instill soldierly acceptance of death in their troops, often by strange means, the results were counterproductive. The tragicomic divisional commander on Mount Fior, General Leone, asks Emilio Lussu "whether or not he loved war." Because he gets a less than enthusiastic reply, he sets out to demonstrate how war ought to be welcomed. Stepping on a heap of stones, he defiantly stands head and shoulders above the parapet of the trench to look at the enemy's position. Four shots ring out but miss him; undeterred, the general remains erect and exposed. When he finally lowers himself with studied indifference, he turns to one of the soldiers, who has watched the performance in disbelief and fear, and tells him: "If you are not afraid . . . do what your general has done." Obligingly the soldier raises himself above the parapet, but the enemy now fires without missing, and a bullet through the chest drops the soldier. "He is a hero," proclaims the satisfied General Leone, "a true hero," and rewards the wounded trooper with a silver coin.[25]

The Italian soldier, no coward, would have faced death bravely like the English under German fire described by Alan Clark had he known, like the English, that he was dying for something or someone he believed in. He needed some reason, like that of "Uncle Francesco," an overage private in Lussu's company, who volunteered for risky nighttime action. He carried pipes filled with nitroglycerin across no-man's-land, placed them beneath the enemy's barbed wire, and blew it up. He crossed no-man's-land every time regiment headquarters asked for volunteers until he was shot and killed on one of the deadly errands. His reason for facing death was the ten lire that headquarters paid each soldier each time he volunteered. "Uncle Francesco," conscripted in 1915 and in the Libyan war four years earlier, was the head of an indigent southern family and the father of five children. At the time of his death his comrades discovered that all the money he made carrying explosives had been sent home to help his family survive. Rightfully, he received no medal for his heroism, for he was a hero only to his family.[26]

Resignation to death was a complex attitude. Lord Moran, the observer and theorist of suffering and courage, wrote that in the Great War the combatant had to choose between succumbing and adjusting to the intimidating presence of death. Lord Moran believed that by adjusting, the soldier mastered death. He "simply could not afford to allow death to hover in the offing as the final mystery; it must be brought to earth and robbed of its disturbing influence, by rough gibes and the touch of ridicule. If it was firmly grasped like a nettle soon there was no sting left in it." And how were the mystery and the sting of death to be mastered? By natural progression: the longer the soldier stayed at the front, the smaller his chance of survival became, and as the odds shortened and "it became plain that death was to be the common lot, [he] thought less of its coming until at last [he] saw no cruelty in its approach." Not only did Lord Moran see no cruelty in the coming of death, he even rationalized it with reassuring serenity as a good thing: "Surely it is a fine free setting forth, this end in the field. It comes to a man in the springtime, before age and disease have soiled his body and the traffic of cities has stained his soul. He has lived his brief manhood among men, knowing what is best in them, and has gone out untouched and undefeated by the petty strife of a world at peace."[27]

The mood of resignation described by Lord Moran had little to do with the reality of the battlefield, where men under the threat of death gave up on life. Robert Graves and Siegfried Sassoon may have been poised in the face of death, but they showed none of Lord Moran's serene acceptance of the inevitable. After five months in the trenches, exposed to the "continual experience of death," Graves felt no more "horror." Deadened in sensibility and dispirited, he no longer cared whether he lived or died.[28] Sassoon wrote that "in a trench one was acclimatized to the notion of being exterminated," but while he was prepared to die, he was neither willing nor happy to do so.

The meaning of the adjustment forced on him by life in the trenches became clear to Sassoon during his convalescence in London in 1917. An air raid on Liverpool Station that left the victims lying bleeding shocked Sassoon and he was unable to respond with soldierly calm. In the trenches, where death was familiar, he had acted with resignation and indifference. But among the peaceful pursuits of the civilized world, death loomed as a fearsome intruder.[29] Sassoon understood that indifference and mental surrender to death helped the soldier at the front, whereas anxiety about survival worsened his chances. Sassoon ascribed the death of a fellow officer to his eagerness to stay alive:

> Somehow I always thought you'd get done in,
> Because you were so desperate keen to live;
> You were all out to try and save your skin,
> Well knowing how much the world had got to give
> . . . .
> So when they told me you'd been left for dead
> I wouldn't believe them, feeling it *must* be true.[30]

At the front the difference between life and death was blotted out; the soldier's existence was a living death, and death often appeared preferable. "One of the strangest states of mind I noticed at the front is a calm preparation for parting from life," in the words of Pinotto Garrone, one of the fallen heroes celebrated by Adolfo Omodeo, in the spring of 1917.[31] Another Italian officer asked himself: "What . . . separates us from death? . . . Almost nothing." Life, far from being a calm preparation for death, was its noisy vestibule: "Death flies above us with an angry, murderous snarl. Now death could snatch us at any moment, now it rejects us, and now it plays the strangest sarabands."[32]

Life besieged by death became a kind of disease: "He who makes war is in the same state of mind as that of the tubercular: he feels the sickness in his bones, he foresees with horror the last day of his life, he knows that his disease may last a long time, but he also knows that he cannot avoid death."[33] For six days of leave from the front, a comrade of Giani Stuparich was willing to detonate explosives beneath the enemy's barbed wire. To those who wondered why he treated his life so cheaply, he replied that he was sure to die on the front anyway. "We," he told his comrades, "are waiting for death."[34] In a less heroic character, resignation to death might take on a tragic mood. On Mount San Michele Carlo Salsa's troops, short of food and water, felt "forgotten by" and "estranged from" the world, and "sad like condemned men," they saw their life "reduced to a waiting for death."[35] By the spring of 1918 life and death have become the same thing for Paul Baumer and his comrades on the Western Front: "We have almost grown accustomed to it; war is a cause of death like cancer and tuberculosis, like influenza and dysentery. The deaths are merely more frequent, more varied and terrible." The men are doomed, and their common fate gives them a tragic sense of belonging to "a great brotherhood," grown "out of the tension and forlornness of death." It gives them "the feeling of solidarity of convicts, and of the desperate loyalty to one another of men condemned to death."[36]

Life at the front was a kind of slavery that made even death attractive, in the view of Sergeant Jean Dartemont in the war novel *La Peur* (Fear). At night, in the trenches of Chemin des Dames, the biting cold makes Dartemont realize that he has been living like a hungry, worn-out beast. He confesses: "Never have I felt so brutalized, so empty of thought as I do now; and I can now understand how the physical exhaustion that both robs human beings of the possibility to think and reduces their concerns to the elementary needs of existence is a powerful means of domination. I now understand why slaves submit so easily." Why, then, Dartemont asks himself, do he and his soldiers "still oppose death" and cling to their worthless existence, when "animal passivity" has turned them into living dead? Death itself would be better.[37]

It would be a mistake to judge as biased and isolated the views expressed in *La peur* by Gabriel Chevallier, a veteran of the Western Front, whose novel is distinguished by "protest against war and against the noble conception of war."[38] In a work less bent on protest and more sophisticated, *Memoirs of a Fox-Hunting Man*, Siegfried Sassoon comes to much the same conclusions. In the spring of 1916 Sassoon was pinned in the cold trenches of the Somme in the midst of a dismal landscape, where "on wet days the trees a mile away were like ash-gray smoke rising from the naked ridges, and it felt very much as if we were at the end of the world"; it had "no relation to the landscape of life." At that point, "I had more or less made up my mind to die; the idea made things easier. In the circumstances there didn't seem to be anything else to be done."[39] The natural environment, violated by war, diminished the value of human life. Sassoon's reason for choosing death over life—the desecration of nature—was less substantial than Sergeant Dartemont's. But the English officer's determination was perhaps stronger, as suggested by the "rabid" heroism he practiced, the risks he took on the battlefield.

The death-fraught environment of the trenches stirred the imagination even of writers loath to represent the reality of war. Edmund Blunden, whom critics accuse of retreating into a pastoral dreamworld, incapable of expressing "outrage at the moral enormities of war,"[40] described the death-like atmosphere of trench life on the Western Front so vividly that the reader is reminded of Barbusse's most realistic pages. Blunden tears down the veil that separates life from death, revealing that the trench environment does not simply evoke death, but is in fact death itself. Schwaben Redoubt, a German stronghold before being taken by the English in the first battle of the Somme, had by the fall of 1916 become a death-trap for the British themselves. It was "an almost obliterated cocoon of trenches in which mud, and death, and life were much the same thing—and there the deep dugouts, which faced the German guns, were cancerous with torn bodies, and to pass an entrance was to gulp poison. . . . Men of the next battalion were found in mud up to the armpits, and their fate was not spoken of; those who found them could not get them out."[41]

Resignation was the only conceivable response for soldiers who believed the war would last indefinitely. When Blunden joined the Royal Sussex battalion in the trenches north of Béthume in May 1916, his first impression in talking to the veterans was "the prevailing sense of the endlessness of the war." "No one," he wrote in *Undertones of War*, "appeared to conceive any end to it."[42] The inability to see an end to the war had nothing to do with ideas about its progress or with the conventional notion of time. It had to do with hopelessness and deadliness. The enormous number of lives and the vast quantity of materiel devoured by battles attested to the destructiveness of this war. If, the soldier reasoned, the war so far had been this destructive and yet rages on, it can only claim more and more lives. Death, not the passing of time, would end the war. In this sense war was endless: it would last till everybody was killed. And when all had died, time would end.

Jules Romain's reflections in *Verdun* help to explain the concept of "endlessness" created by the war's destructiveness. On the eve of one of the most bloody battles of the Great War, the novel's protagonist Fabre, views the coming clash against the background of the battles the French fought in 1915, battles "more noted for slaughter than for accomplishment,"[43] and he foresees the cost of the imminent action, its futility, and its destructive impact on the soldier's psyche. In the second half of 1915 the French troops, Fabre argues, "had been told so often that this time they were going to finish the job, and all there was to show for it was another lot of lies. They'd be fools indeed if they went on believing what they were told. Then there were all the mistakes that had come to light in the course of the offensive; imperfect preparations: too much wire left undestroyed, too many machine guns in concrete emplacements which the artillery had failed to silence, just in the very places where there oughtn't to have been any. . . . The failure of the offensive . . . had shaken their confidence. . . . Now they preferred to conclude that if victory couldn't be achieved in conditions . . . regarded as almost perfect, then it could never be achieved at all. There was no reason why this unnatural war should ever stop, or rather it would only stop when everybody, on both sides, had been killed. . . . The soldiers were beginning to think that they were in for a life sentence. The end of the ordeal would come only with the end of their lives."[44]

The all-out offensives, the reckless dispatch with which men were thrown into battles, fed the "prevailing sense of the endlessness of war." The lack of success only lengthened war indefinitely, while the mounting casualties increased the certainty of death. Captain Thompson arouses only skepticism when he announces to the soldiers of Frederic Manning's company that an imminent offensive by the infantry will be preceded by such an artillery bombardment that "it is not expected that the enemy will offer any very serious resistance." Besides, the captain says "men are strictly forbidden to stop for the purpose of assisting the wounded." Some of the troops feel that they are being taken "for a lot of bloody kids"; they have seen before the heavy losses on the barbed wire of the enemy line. Headquarters has given no reassuring sign that the artillery barrage would eliminate the enemy machine guns and barbed wire before the next assault, and the directive to ignore the wounded in the field would surely increase the casualties.

The author of the directive may have been, as the soldiers surmise, a "bloody fool," but he had a purpose in mind. He wanted, Frederic Manning's comrades believe, to destroy in them the resistance to limitless losses: "We all know that there must be losses, you can't expect to take a trench without some casualties; but they [headquarters] . . . go on from saying that losses are unavoidable, to thinking they are necessary, and from that, to thinking that they don't matter."[45] If losses do not matter, then neither do lives and the troops can expect only death. "And the War won't end for at least two years; / But we've got stacks of men," wrote Sassoon;[46] as long as the supply of men to be sacrificed on the battlefield was ample, it mattered not how soon the war ended.

Superior officers felt the sense of an endless war and the coming of the holocaust no less than the troops. After conferring with General Cadorna on September 1, 1917, about a battle in which the Italians attacked on the Bainsizza Plateau, his aide, Colonel Gatti, wrote in despair in his diary: "My impression . . . is that this war is much too far from the end!" It appeared to be a "machine built to work for eternity." Gatti was crushed: "I feel that something is collapsing inside me; I will not be able to endure this war, none of us will be able to; it is too gigantic, it is truly limitless, it will crush us all."[47] The action on the Bainsizza was the eleventh of the twelve battles of the Isonzo—the last in the series of futile offensives (the twelfth would be the defensive, losing battle of Caporetto). Despite the high number of casualties—one hundred fifty thousand men in less than two months—the battle of the Bainsizza neither broke the Austrian line of defense, its objective, nor wrested any territory from the enemy.

In the words of a historian of the Great War, the eleventh battle of the Isonzo offered the "clearest demonstration" that the war of attrition, no matter how large the materiel employed, exhausted both of the contenders without reaching the goal that the Italian General Staff had sought for two years—a breakthrough in the Austrian defensive line.[48] Despite the failure of the strategy of attrition, General Cadorna's thinking showed no sign of change. During the eleventh battle Gatti describes him as "tranquil, serene, rested . . . happy," and "made of iron," unbending. "He speaks slowly," Gatti noted, "but he is sure of himself: he sees nothing but his own thought. . . . Everything that others say or do glides away from Cadorna like the sea wave from the rock. It leaves no trace."[49] No wonder Colonel Gatti feared that war waged by such a general would grind on forever and "crush" everybody!

At the front, death appeared daily in a variety of forms—the maimed bodies, the shell-shocked, the unburied, rotting corpses and their stench. Death was not "unreal" and "incomprehensible," as a student of both world wars states;[50] it was quite real and always very near, and the soldier who managed to escape it was regarded as a "God."[51] Wilfred Owen, whom Dylan Thomas styled the "prophet in death's country"[52] for his keen perception of existence on the Western Front, spoke of the inescapable intrusiveness of "comrade Death":

> Out there, we've walked quite frequently with Death
> Sat down and eaten with him, cool and bland,
> . . . .
> We've sniffed the green thick odour of his breath,
> . . . .
> He's spat at us with bullets and he's coughed
> Shrapnel. We chorussed when he sang aloft;
> We whistled while he shaved us with his scythe.
> Oh, Death was never enemy of ours!
> We laughed at him, we leagued with him, old chum.[53]

By its closeness and familiarity alone, death could conquer the soldier. "When you hear of or see the death of one of those who fought by your side and lived exactly the same life," Barbusse wrote, "you receive a direct blow in the flesh before even understanding. It is truly as if you heard of your own destruction."[54]

After living in "death's country," and suffering the inner death described by Barbusse, soldiers came to wish for their own end. After the victory at Akaba in July 1917, when the Arabs had plundered the Turkish troops, T.E. Lawrence paused to survey the battlefield. The corpses he saw fascinated him, and death beckoned: "The dead men looked wonderfully beautiful. The night was shining gently down, softening them into new ivory. . . . The corpses seemed flung so pitifully on the ground, huddled anyhow in low heaps. Surely if straightened they would be comfortable at last. So I put them all in order, one by one, very wearied myself, and longing to be one of these quiet ones, not of the restless, noisy, aching mob up the valley." Lawrence longed to be "with death, whether [he] won or lost, waiting to end the history."[55] Another emotion—shame for his egotistical role in the Arab revolt—helped Lawrence shape his death wish into a romantic and peaceful experience.[56]

But the death wish usually assailed the soldier in a more brutal and terrorizing way than it did Lawrence at Akaba. Abuse, hunger, and excessive risk made the common soldier feel a sense of doom about his life. After a series of unsuccessful attacks, some of Captain Lussu's exhausted soldiers in their dugout tried one night in the summer of 1916 to guess whether or not they would be sent against the enemy's line again the next day. One of the soldiers argues that another attack is unlikely because neither chocolate nor cognac, the troops' "gasoline," have been sent up from the rear. But another points out that the policy of supplying the troops with the ingredients of bravery before an assault may have changed. "You will see," this soldier warns, "that these brigands [headquarters] will have us killed without chocolate and without cognac." The likely deprivation of these treats reminds the soldiers of the lack of even basic nourishment, and headquarters' neglect strikes them as a deliberate effort at driving them to throw their lives away. "They [headquarters] want us hungry, thirsty, and desperate. So they make us loathe life"[57] and seek annihilation.

The bombardment or the assault that brutally cut men down made the survivors feel that death was inescapable. That acute observer of men's behavior under fire on the Italian front, Father Gemelli, wrote that under a prolonged bombardment the combatant "regarded himself as if he were already dead, as if he were finished." The soldier repudiated life and welcomed death, for death "appeared to him as a liberation" from the terrifying experience of the barrage,[58] from "the huge black dogs of hell / Leaping full-mouthed, in murderous pursuit."[59] Death was the welcome exit from that hell.[60]

The attitude described by Father Gemelli must have been

common among combatants, for it shows up where one would least expect it—in fearless, bloodthirsty Ernst Junger, the German Storm Trooper officer who went on fighting till the end of the war despite fourteen wounds and "twenty punctures" in his body. At Langemarck in the summer of 1917 heavy French shelling forced him and his men to lie close to one another in a narrow, crowded ditch at the side of a road. The ground "rocked like a ship's deck under hit after hit" and shrapnel picked off Junger's soldiers until both he and his troops "were ready for the end." Nonetheless, he writes, he chewed his pipe and, succeeded "in philosophizing [himself] into courage." What kind of courage? Not the courage to stand up to the destruction around him, not the guts to defy death, but the urge to call for death. "I repeated several times to myself," Junger recalled, "a saying of Ariosto, 'A great heart cares nothing for death when it comes, so long as it be glorious.' "[61]

Under the circumstances death could not possibly be glorious, only a useful means of escape. Yet Junger appealed to glory to justify the wish whose fulfillment would have freed him of the terror of bombardment. "What was hard to do" under the barrage, Lieutenant Ghisalberti, a veteran of the Carso, wrote, "was to lie down, because lying down meant that the soldier was paralyzed, that he had to feel the fall of the blows, those of the heavy artillery, those of the light artillery, and those of the machine guns. Lying down meant that the soldier was unable to move either forward or backward, it meant that he had to wait. Wait for what? For what I myself asked for . . . 'the deliverer bullet.' "[62]

The true aim of the soldier on the offensive, on his way through no-man's-land toward the enemy line, was not the taking of the line. His true aim was ridding himself of the tension and terror that gripped him. And death offered him the means. "Let us all die, but let us get over with Hill 121," the men and officers of Gino Stuparich's battalion felt after bloody but futile attacks on the Austrian-held Monfalcone stronghold at the beginning of the war. They wished for death, to spare themselves more attacks and more suffering.[63] Kurt Peterson, a young philosophy student from Berlin, sent on a second, vain night assault on Dixmude early in the war, was pinned to the ground by French machine-gun fire while "death hissed and howled" about him. "One dreads death," he wrote home of the experience, which made of him an "old man," nevertheless "one could . . . long for it through horror at this kind of death."[64]

The fear of showing cowardice—the fear of fear itself—intensified the death wish. Living with terror when courage could not be mustered was, as Lieutenant Ghisalberti recalled, the supreme agony. "No one who has not known the Carso . . . can understand how fear gripped man's throat. . . . The general staff's reports can't convey the real sense of the war the way the men who fought it felt it. The reports deal with both the important and insignificant events of the war, but not with the struggle against fear." The assault offered an end to that struggle. For Ghisalberti the assault was "the flight forward": When fear got hold of the soldier, he decided that it was better to stand up, run toward the enemy, and die than to hug the ground in fear.[65] The soldier who ran across no-man's-land to storm the enemy's position was impelled by the "atrocious physical spasm" of fear, not by his eagerness to liquidate the enemy. Courage has nothing to do with the attacker's drive, explained Lieutenant Attilio Frescura. Courage belongs only to the deserter, who runs backward even though he knows that if caught he will face prosecution and the inevitable loss of life he is trying to save. In contrast, the soldier who storms the enemy line flees toward his liberation: he "has given up life and runs forward screaming, killing, and winning, both against the enemy and against himself. His forward rush means the end of his spasmodic nightmare, the end . . . of his torment," of a life made unlivable by fear.

This release explains why the soldier, in the grip of fear and of the suicidal impulse, "howls in an unforgettable manner" when he goes over the top.[66] The howl heard by Lieutenant Frescura on the Italian front was the same that Jean Bernier heard on the Western Front: the signal of the troops' conscious rush to self-destruction. When Favigny's company attacks in the final action of *La percée* (The break-through), Bernier writes that "a hideous, obscene clamour arose. It swelled and drowned even the sound of the machine guns; a furious retch of fathomless horror, as though far off, away from their empty bodies, they [the troops] were vomiting forth their broken, tortured lives. Ah . . . ah . . . ah. . . . The surging howl continued, triumphant over all."[67]

The death wish shaped by the moment of assault grew out of the cumulative strain and agony of life at the front; it came as liberation from degradation. "He wished he were one of the skeletons lying on Hill 91"; he wished he were "an anonymous body among the corpses lying outside in the street": this is how George Winterbourne, the protagonist of Richard Aldington's *Death of a Hero*, felt on the eve of his last action. He wished for death out of self-contempt and despair. He was at the very end of his endurance; lice infested his body and boils covered his back; Winterbourne, an artist, could no longer find enjoyment even in beauty, and the failure of his esthetic faculty hit him hard. "A wrecked man," he "moved through impressions like a man hallucinated. And every incident seemed to beat on his brain, Death, Death, Death." Degradation paves his way toward death, in two senses: first, Winterbourne loses a part of himself—his humanity shrinks, and second, the loss blinds him to his fate; he loses consciousness of the boundary between life and death, and marches to his own destruction oblivious of himself.

When the battle, the last one fought by the armies on the Western Front, began and the attack unfolded, Winterbourne "saw his Runner stagger and fall as a shell burst. . . . Then his Corporal disappeared, blown to pieces by a direct hit . . . Jameson dead; Halliwell dead; Sergeant Morton, Taylor and Fish, dead in a little group . . . Winterbourne's second Runner was hit, and lay groaning." At this point, where death sucks lives from all around him, he translates his impulse to self-destruct into reality: "Something seemed to break in Winterbourne's head. He felt he was going mad, and sprang to his feet. The line of bullets smashed across his chest like a savage steel whip," and his death wish is fulfilled.[68]

Aldington's novel may not be, as a critic noted, a work wrought with great art.[69] But it stands apart, because it portrays what no other novel of the Great War, except Lussu's *Un anno sull'altipiano,* does: the fulfillment of what General J.F.C. Fuller styled one of the aspirations of the general staffs of World War I: increasing the eagerness to face death to the point where the combatant would throw his life away.[70]

The death wish that grew out of the experience at the front sometimes led to an end less dramatic, though no less welcome, than Winterbourne's. The heroes of both Aldington's and Remarque's novels die just before the end of the war. The timing dramatizes the choice that Aldington and Remarque made for their protagonists: death over life at the moment when the return to civilian life, to real life, is imminent. Estrangement from humanity brought both Winterbourne and Baumer to the point of no return, barring them from regaining what they lost. The spectacle of comrades destroyed one by one intensified and actualized Winterbourne's death wish, and his was an angry death. Baumer instead died peacefully in a trench at the end of *All Quiet on the Western Front*: "He had fallen forward and lay on the earth as though sleeping. Turning him over one saw that he could not have suffered long; his face had an expression of calm, as though almost glad that the end had come."[71] Death both marks the reversion to the state of peace and innocence in which twenty-year-old Baumer lived before the war, and delivers him from the burden of a meaningless life. The smile that breaks through the mask of death shows the fulfillment of his death wish.

Baumer's "happy" release contrasts with the "reluctant" death of his friend and comrade Franz Kemmerich, which takes up most of the novel's opening.[72] Devastated by gangrene, Kemmerich in a field hospital suffers a drawn-out death, his emotional pain conveyed by the physical details of his debility toward the end: "His lips have fallen away, his mouth has become larger, his teeth stick out and look as though they were made of chalk. The flesh melts, the forehead bulges more prominently, the cheekbones protrude. The skeleton is working its way through." At the same time a desperate but vain desire to live possesses him. "The whole world," Baumer muses as he impotently witnesses his friend's end, "ought to pass by his bed and say: 'That is Franz Kemmerich, nineteen and a half years old, he does not want to die. Let him not die!' " But Kemmerich "is entirely alone now with his little life of nineteen years, and cries because it leaves him."[73]

So death encapsulates *All Quiet on the Western Front*, and the progression from a dreaded death to a welcome one underscores the novel's shift from concern for the preservation of life to a yearning for death. In a world at peace there will be no place for those who come back from the death zone: "We will be superfluous even to ourselves, we will grow older, a few will adapt themselves, some others will merely submit, and most will be bewildered; the years will pass by and in the end we shall fall into ruin." Baumer and his comrades, unfit for life because their youth is burned out by death and killing, are consigned to a kind of limbo, having lost their souls even before the gun destroyed their bodies: "I am young, I am twenty years old," Baumer reflects shortly before his end, "yet I know nothing of life but despair, death, fear. . . . What would our fathers do if we suddenly stood up and came before them and proffered our account? What do they expect if a time ever comes when the war is over? Through the years our business has been killing—it was our first calling in life. Our knowledge of life is limited to death."[74] The poetry of the Great War depicts the impulse to self-destruct in those who, like Baumer and his comrades, lived in the orbit of death:

> Take me under thy wing, O death.
> I am tired, I am cold.
> . . . .
> Take me, carry me hence
> And let me sleep.
> . . . .
> The beast in man is again on the trail
> Swinging his arms and sniffing the air for blood.[75]

The death wish was instead directed toward others in response to the death of close comrades. The survivor vented his anger, his spirit of revenge, in trying to kill the enemy—a compulsive behavior captured in one of Sassoon's poem:

> When dawn was grey I stood with the Dead.
> And my slow heart said: "You must kill, you must kill:
> "Soldier, soldier, morning is red."[76]

Sassoon himself obeyed that compulsion to kill when his lance corporal was shot the first day of the Somme offensive, in July 1916. The two of them were on an exploratory raid into Mametz Wood, and, the poet recalls, "I felt adventurous and it seemed as if Kendle and I were having great fun together." A bullet between Lance Corporal Kendle's eyes suddenly ended the sense of fun, which was quickly replaced by belligerency in the survivor. "All feelings tightened and contracted to a single intention—to settle that sniper. . . . I had lost my temper with the man who had shot Kendle." He rushes the enemy trench, hurling bombs all the while at the Germans, who flee for their lives. Sassoon conquers the enemy position single-handedly and he exults: "Idiotically elated I stood there with my finger in my right ear and emitted a series of 'view-holloas'."[77]

The killing of Martlow, "the kid," in the last pages of Manning's *The Middle Parts of Fortune* lends more savagery to Bourne's drive against the Germans than did Kendle's death to Sassoon. With "consuming hate" for the enemies and "exultant cruelty" within himself, Bourne throws himself against their position screaming: "Kill the bastards! Kill the bloody fucking swines! Kill them!"[78]

The release of such pent-up anger often left the combatant low instead of giving him a sense of accomplishment. When Wilfred Owen wrote that "power was on us as we slashed bones bare / Not to feel sickness or remorse of murder," he evoked the ease, the intensity, and the cruelty with which the soldier killed on the battlefield when anger or revenge drove him. But Owen also knew that, although the heat of the battle and revengeful fury might spare the killer sickness and remorse, his act robbed him of his sanity and rationality: "Merry it was to laugh there— / Where death becomes absurd and life absurder."[79] Slashing "bones bare" emptied both death and life of any meaning.

"In a madness born of the horror of Tafas," an Arab village where women and children were massacred by a column of retreating Turkish soldiers a few hours before T.E. Lawrence and his guerrillas got there, "We killed and killed . . . even blowing in the heads of the fallen and of the animals; as though their death and running blood could slake our agony." Against those Turks who put up resistance, the Arabs fought "like devils, the sweat blurring their eyes, dust parching their throats, while the flame of cruelty and revenge which was burning in their bodies so twisted them that their hands could hardly shoot." For the only time in the desert war Lawrence at Tafas gave the "no prisoners" order, and two hundred captives taken by the Arabs were herded together and machine-gunned.[80] Lawrence regarded mass killing as fitting punishment for Turkish savagery. But his conscience never came to terms with what he did at Tafas; the role he played in the bloodshed tormented him and generated those "forbidden or unacceptable . . . impulses" that in the aftermath of the war made his life "absurd" and degraded.[81]

The death of comrades, anger, and the spirit of revenge intensified the death wish of the survivor, and the combatant spontaneously felt the impulse to kill the enemy.[82] If, for whatever reason, the sources of aggressiveness were absent, the impulse to kill was missing too. One early morning at Casara Zebio, Captain Lussu crawled close to the Austrian trench seeking to discover the location of a small-caliber gun whose fire had made misery for his men. Instead of the gun he sighted an Austrian officer, only a few yards away, who was drinking coffee and smoking a cigarette among his soldiers. Lussu aimed his rifle at the officer's head, but could not bring himself to shoot. "It was enough for me to pull the trigger," Lussu recalled, "and the Austrian officer would have fallen to the ground. The certainty that his life depended on my will made me hesitate. A man was standing in front of me. A man! A man!" The Italian captain felt that he could not shoot a man from such a short distance, as if he were a boar. It occurred to him then that "to make war is one thing, but to kill a man is another," and that to kill a man the way he was about to do "meant murder." He lowered his rifle, telling himself: "It will not be you who will kill a man this way."[83]

The front made the presence of death continual and pervasive, and this presence generated a cynical disregard for life, a contempt far more widespread and unsettling than the individual death wish implied. By 1917 Georges Duhamel, an enlisted army doctor who served for fifty-one months on the Western Front, had performed two thousand operations and cared for four thousand wounded[84]—an overwhelming experience of death. He realized that in the civilian world death was separated from life, "talked about . . . covertly," and regarded as both painful and indecent. It was therefore disguised by symbols and announced in laborious paraphrases marked by a kind of shame. But in war, Duhamel found, death has become "closely bound up with the things of life . . . it has become a thing so ordinary that it no longer causes us to suspend our usual activities, as it used to do: we eat and drink beside the dead, we sleep amidst the dying, we laugh and sing in the company of corpses. . . . Like the king who showed himself at his toilet, Death is still powerful, but it has become familiar and . . . degraded."[85] But the experience with the men who suffered and whom Duhamel cared for in the military hospitals led him to believe in man's ability to rise above misery. So he refrained from drawing conclusions about the debasing effect of unnatural familiarity with death, conclusions that would deny the human dignity that Duhamel saw in his patients.

Another French writer, Jules Romains, did what Duhamel was reluctant to do; he depicted the result of living in the midst of death. Lieutenant Jerphanion, the leading character of *Verdun*, writes to his friend Pierre Jallez that at the front the soldier spends his days "next door" to the dead, "or constantly meeting the signs of their proximity," and thus becomes unnaturally familiar with death. Such familiarity has suppressed pity and grief in the living and has fostered instead cynical unconcern about dying. The combatants "are delighted at the thought that they need no longer approach life with kid gloves." They even "seem . . . relieved at being freed from the particular attitude of respect for human life" that belongs to civilized man; they "derive a sort of gutter satisfaction from treating life . . . like so much dirt." When the stench of the putrefying corpses around the trenches reaches the nostrils of the soldier, he expresses impotent revulsion toward the dead, as one would when "the sanitary men were emptying a neighbouring cesspool." At the front "human sensibilities" are deadened, "the bonds of sentiment" are destroyed, and, as a result, life is devalued. "The irreverent laughter induced in us by the spectacle of life" destroyed and rotting, explains the French lieutenant, "prevents us from taking our own individual lives seriously. Men . . . are seen to be like a shoal of fish or cloud of locusts swarming to destruction. The individual man is less than nothing. . . . The act of clinging to life is merely so much extra and useless trouble. We just let ourselves be swept along." The death of sensibility and feeling betrays something graver: man's reversion to a primitive, savage state. "This . . . is the one irreparable loss," concludes Jerphanion. "It has taken civilization centuries of patient fumbling to teach men that life, their own and that of others, is something sacred. Well, it's been so much work thrown away. We shan't, you'll see, get back to that attitude in a hurry."[86]

Jules Romains's estimate of the effect of death on the survivors echoes the thought of a work written under the impression of the extraordinary destructiveness of World War I, Freud's *Reflections on War and Death*.[87] Six months after the beginning of the war, when people were dying "no longer one by one, but in large numbers, often ten thousand in one day," Freud questioned how twentieth-century man, the product of centuries of civilization, could do so much killing. He explained the butchery that was taking place in the battlefields as the unleashing of the primitive murderous instinct that civilization had managed to tame, but that war reawakened. In the consciousness of primitive man, Freud reasoned, the division between life and death was precarious. Primitive man had no respect for life, and killed frequently, filling "the primitive history of mankind . . . with murder." That murderousness is reflected in many a religion's "assumption of a primal guilt . . . a blood guilt"—the killing of "the primal father of the primitive horde." The commandment "Thou shalt not kill" is an injunction that "makes it certain that we are descended from an endlessly long chain of generations of murderers, whose love of murder was in their blood." It took mankind centuries to formulate the prohibition against killing and to overcome the murderous instinct. The respect paid to that commandment is "an acquisition of the history of man" and "the hereditary possession" of modern peoples. Yet war now reasserts the primacy of death, Freud concluded. War "strips off the later deposits of civilization and allows the primitive man in us to reappear. . . . It stamps all strangers as enemies whose death we ought to cause or wish; it counsels us to rise above the death of those whom we love."[88]

Freud's thought struggled against the perversion by which death was gaining ascendancy over life, but at the same time other European intellectuals extolled what Freud deplored. Italians were especially vociferous in their praise of, and incitement to, dying. Their contempt for the common man, their disappointment in the achievements of the Risorgimento, and their wish for the Italian people to atone for their national failures, fostered their penchant for death. Before the common people were sent to the front to fight and to die, Giovanni Papini wrote, "they lived just because they happened to be born . . . ate to live . . . worked to eat, and . . . cursed their work, but did not have the guts to do away with their life." Once they are killed, Papini continued, these wretches, "carrions, embraced in death," are not even worthy of remembrance. It is indeed a blessing for everyone that so many "dislikable, lowbrow, rascals, idiots . . . useless beasts" have left the world.[89]

Giuseppe de Robertis, like Papini a star contributor to *La voce*, thought that the common people should be thankful for the opportunity to fight and die on the battlefield. Death conferred upon them some dignity, which they lacked entirely before the war; they were nothing but "third rate men, wretched, cowards, hooligans, mafiosi, meddlers."[90] Many of those who died in the war were the dregs of society, who did not even know what they were fighting for. Considering the wretchedness of the Italian people, "what better thing could they have done in life," Giuseppe Prezzolini asked, than to have been killed at the front? In this way they took themselves out of circulation and at the same time did something good for the country.[91] Such people do not even deserve an honorable death, the novelist Riccardo Bacchelli felt. When as a combatant he saw the Italian soldiers fight and die on the battlefields, he thought they died only to obey orders, and their death, like their life, was worthless. "Alone, they kill and die" a miserable death: "Without absolution from sin, without any help, without any farewell." No one cries over their unburied bodies and no religious rite is performed. "The only ceremony that marks their passing away is the putrefaction of their unburied bodies, whose penetrating stench spreads swiftly everywhere."[92]

Corrado Alvaro, a novelist and a veteran like Bacchelli, felt that war was an appropriate ending to the unremitting "pain of living" of the common people of Italy. For generations they have fought against poverty and have often known the victory of death over life. In war they meet death as something familiar. They recognize in it the hand of the same destiny that has always ruled them, and they submit to it without asking questions.[93] In his imagination the artist Ardengo Soffici consigns the troops of his battalion to death even before they engage in combat. An infantryman officer, he sees the troops, lying on the ground waiting for the signal to attack Mount Kobilek, as an "expanse of bodies," a "mass of flesh" produced by the "holocaust of the battle."[94]

The image that Gabriele D'Annunzio creates, like Soffici's mass of living soldiers possessed by death, has more imaginative power. Behind the front at Versa, D'Annunzio observes the diverse physical characteristics of the soldiers that listen to mass in the field. The configuration of the human skull leads him to brood about "the skeleton waiting inside the flesh, imitating the gestures of the flesh . . . a prisoner." The skull, D'Annunzio senses, waits to be released from the flesh that holds it prisoner. For D'Annunzio the soldiers are "heads already touched by death, already marked by the Tireless Worker. A mass of flesh to be slaughtered, well prepared cannon-fodder."[95]

In D'Annunzio there was more to death than contempt for the common man and yearning for national glory. D'Annunzio worshipped death; he courted it, and flaunted his delight. Enlisting at the age of fifty-two, he fought on land, at sea, and in the air. He flew over Pola, Trieste, and Vienna to drop bombs and propaganda leaflets; he conceived, and took part in, the raid on the impenetrable haven of Buccari and the torpedoing of a large Austrian warship; and he fought with the infantry on the Isonzo for the conquest of the Veliki and Faiti peaks.

At his ripe age, D'Annunzio was no novice to the cult of death. In his novel *The Triumph of Death*, published twenty years before the war, Giorgio Aurispa, though young, handsome, and beloved, confesses his unfitness for life: "I do not belong to myself—my one end and aim is to escape from myself. I am like a man condemned to stand upon an oscillating and perilous surface, who perpetually feels the ground give way beneath his feet. . . . I have the most burning desire to live, to bring all my powers into rhythmical subordination, to feel myself a complete and harmonious whole. Instead of which I die daily; each day a part of my life slips from me through countless invisible fissures. . . . What is it that is wanting in me? Who then controls that part of my consciousness which is forever eluding me but which nevertheless, I feel instinctively, is indispensable to my existence. Or is that part of me already dead—and death alone can restore it to me? That is the true solution of the mystery—death attracts me."[96] The lure of death in this early novel found restrained expression in the work of D'Annunzio's next twenty years, and returned as a central theme only after the Great War.

When the poet-warrior's seaplane crashed on a sandbank near Venice in January of 1916, his head struck the mounted machine gun and he was blinded for several hours. He eventually lost the sight in his right eye entirely, but a year of care and convalescence saved the left one. His eyes bandaged, D'Annunzio spent this year in immobility, brooding over his comrades' and his own war deeds. And so *Notturno* (Nocturne) was born. In its first pages, D'Annunzio reaches back to the death of Giuseppe Miraglia, his favorite pilot, who perished at the end of 1915 in an airplane crash. When the pilot's body was brought to Venice for the funeral, D'Annunzio visited the mortuary, where the corpse of his comrade worked powerfully on the poet's imagination.

"I set my mouth into the fullness of death," D'Annunzio recalls after he first visited Miraglia's remains. "My grief was slackened by the sight of the coffin as a beast's hunger is quenched at the manger." He quickly realizes that he "could not take any other food." He leaves, then returns to the chamber "to feed" again on the dead: "The corpse is stretched on a tiny wheel-bed. The head is bandaged. The mouth shut, the damaged right eye, livid. The broken right jaw begins to swell. The face is olive-brown. . . . The swollen upper lip protrudes. Cotton wads fill the nostrils." People move in and out of the death-chamber, but the spectacle of death has transfixed D'Annunzio. When someone tries to take him away, he resists. "I cannot move, I cannot get up."

He spends the whole night in the chamber and, before leaving in the morning, he lifts the sheet from the corpse to look at its "swollen face," at "the tightening mouth," at "the brown color turning darker." He returns that night to resume the contemplation of death and decay. He looks at "the face of the dead man," he sees "the swollen, bleeding nose, the nostrils full of cotton . . . a cotton gag hiding the mouth. The dark hue is getting darker." The next day, when "the smell of death in the chamber has become unbearable," D'Annunzio goes out, comes back, leaves again. In the evening he returns to find that the flowers and the furniture have been removed from the chamber. Alone, he confronts the corpse and with a shiver notices a dark spot on the floor under the wheel-bed: "The corpse is breaking up. I see the hands moving apart, the bare feet quivering, the head extending itself under its own weight. . . . The hands are yellow, the face is almost black, like that of a half-breed."[97]

The power with which death attracts the poet in *Notturno* compels him to trace the pull to its origin. The visit of the poet's mother and a family servant, who brings to the convalescent D'Annunzio a live quail, triggers in *Notturno* a searing remembrance. In a flashback to childhood, the poet remembers watching quails held in narrow cages, which rubbed their little heads on the bars in a vain attempt to escape, cutting themselves to the bone. "Those little naked skulls, those bleeding beaks," the poet writes, "gave me a sudden urge to flee, or to kill myself."[98]

At the yearly slaughter of the fat pigs by farmhands in the courtyard of the home near Pescara in Abruzzi, the child was so terrorized by death that the fear almost killed him. When the throats of the pigs were cut, the animals squealed in their agony. Inside the house the child heard the squeals, and horror seized him. "Horror," D'Annunzio recalls, "chased me from one room to another. Life frightened me, as if it stalked me with a knife in its hand. I hid in a corner, my face turned to the wall, and a hand pressing my convulsed mouth. Sobbing shook me all night long. The next morning I looked white, white as if a vein of my neck had been cut open."

The reminiscence surprises D'Annunzio because he realizes that death repelled him as a child, whereas it lures him as a man. The memory is also a signal that the abhorrence he once felt for bloodshed and death still lives and generates the impulse to redeem himself. "Why," he asks after recalling his two childhood experiences of death, "does this temptation to break loose at once from every cruelty and every horror come to me from so far back?"[99] But for D'Annunzio there will be no turning back.

Death compels D'Annunzio in a different way than it did the Futurists and Vorticists, the European intellectuals who questioned the values of contemporary civilization and who sought to create new ones through the destruction of the old. In his last poem Guillaume Apollinaire, recovering from wounds but very near the end of life, sings of death as a triumph:

> I have at last detached myself
> From all natural things
> . . . .

And what no one has ever touched
. . . .
I have touched, I have felt
. . . .
And I have explored what no man
Can imagine in any way.[100]

Wyndham Lewis, a British artillery officer on the Western Front, admired war's destructive power; he felt that "the fearful flashing of a monstrous cannonade" in a dark night made war "romantic." He also found impressive "the agitation of the mental field within the organism marked down to be destroyed."[101] Tommaso Marinetti held death in war a precious thing: "We prefer violent death and we glorify it as the only thing worthy of man, beast of prey." For Marinetti, to die in war was man's supreme goal: "Blood, be it known, holds neither value nor beauty unless it is freed by iron and by fire from the arteries that imprison it."[102] Death, then, is to be loved: "Let us love war and let us savor it like gourmands as long as it lasts," urged Papini. "War," he added, "is frightening, and just because it is frightening, tremendous, terrible, and destructive, we must love it with all our masculine heart."[103]

D'Annunzio shows none of the uplifting quality that strikes the reader of Lewis and Apollinaire, despite the cult of death embodied in their words. D'Annunzio's penchant for death shows the destructive traits of both a Marinetti and a Papini—and something else besides. In the reminiscence about the dead comrade in *Notturno*, D'Annunzio approaches death as the worm approaches putrefying flesh—he feeds on it, thrives on it, and revels in it. He savors the negation of life, and because in death he finds his natural habitat, he inverts values and he reduces life to death: "Death is . . . like life . . . intoxicating, promising, transfiguring."[104] Other writer-warriors of D'Annunzio's cast of mind inverted values, too. Ernst Junger thought that as the soldier got closer to death, a kind of decadent bliss swept his life away: the "earthly light shows up most brilliantly, as in Boccaccio's pictures of it outside the gates of plague-stricken Florence, as in the love of consumptives, or as a Bacchanal on a sinking ship."[105] And the skirmish at Charleroi convinced Pierre Drieu La Rochelle that "there is no difference between life and death," that "death is not nothingness," but "the continuation of life." After leading his company in a charge against the enemy, he realized that life and death were inseparable: "I wanted to live and die at the same time. I could not wish to live without wanting to die. I could not suddenly ask for a full life, without asking at the same time for death, without accepting destruction."[106]

But D'Annunzio goes beyond reducing life to death: he reduces death to animality, and exults in the degradation. The flashback to Giuseppe Miraglia, riveted by the decomposing corpse of the pilot, excludes any esteem for love of country or heroism. In the grisly care and the morbid persistence with which he portrays Miraglia's remains, the poet degrades death. The depiction of the corpse of another fallen comrade, Giovanni Federico, a twenty-year-old sailor from D'Annunzio's native region, Abruzzi, throws more light on the poet's peculiar perception of death. Even though the youth's death touches him, D'Annunzio expresses no regret or affectionate feeling for Federico. In *Notturno* he writes instead that Giovanni "is laid out like one of those animals that the butcher has quartered on the slaughterhouse's chopping block. His soul is divine in proportion as his body is brutish. Only the shreds of his rough shirt cover him; and his bare genitals increase the revulsion and the misery." The sight exalts the poet: "Heroism, blood, death . . . put me in a state of grace appropriate to receive and to lengthen the unheard melody . . . of the divine war." The degradation that the poet confers on death engulfs his own life. After his imagination has fed on Giovanni Federico's body, D'Annunzio realizes that he, too, has become an animal, perhaps the same animal that crawled around Miraglia's corpse in the Venetian mortuary: "My grief is full of blood. My dreams are full of blood. Every thought of mine is soaked with blood. Sometimes my past repulses me and bleeds like a slaughterhouse filled with quartered beasts hanging from the walls."[107]

D'Annunzio will keep worshipping at the altar of bloodshed and death even after *Notturno*. In *Il libro ascetico della giovane Italia* (The ascetic book of young Italy) he recalls the battle fought for a height on the Carso, the Veliki, where neither heroism nor the spirit of victory fires his imagination; the triumph of death does. Death, not the soldiers, conquers the height. The attack on the Veliki, D'Annunzio writes, "was a celestial ascent. Its strength was born out of death. Death was carried upward by the fervor and the uproar [of the attack] like a plebeian wench who, taken by the fever of a riot, sings at the top of her voice the raging song. The fallen were no obstacle, but the spring [of the attack]. The wounded were bloodshed's standard bearers."[108] The decimation of the infantry brigade Catanzaro at Santa Maria La Longa in July 1917, the worst mass execution performed by the Italian army during the war, gave D'Annunzio another opportunity to celebrate death and revel in its horror. The justice or injustice of the deed—the slaughter of soldiers from an impoverished southern region whose brigade had earned a gold medal for heroism on the slopes of the Hermada—leaves the poet indifferent. A few hours after witnessing the execution outside the cemetery's walls, he returns to the site. There he finds the "helmets, shreds of brain swarming with flies, and dried up rivulets of blood," but the corpses have been removed. In the cemetery he finds the remains, which he describes as a lover would describe parts of the loved one's body: "I saw the pale ears, the hollow hands. . . . I fancied the lean ankles held by the wool of the worn out bands, I fancied the crushed skulls lying under some tree branches."[109]

D'Annunzio's encounter with the dead at Santa Maria La Longa yields the confession that communing with death has become for him a way of life: "For many weeks I have been living with them [the dead], I live dying and coming back to life in them, I lie down along them; or I raise myself up on my elbows to recognize them, to examine them, to look at them again; or I hold them in my arms. . . . How long have I lain alongside the dead! How many nights have I kept vigil in my cemetery of Ronchi and in that of Cosala!" D'Annunzio, now knitted to death, calls himself "the dead's firstborn."[110]

Pulled by a rabid nationalism demanding blood and a decadent genius warping human values, D'Annunzio could "see in the world nothing but matter, and in man nothing but animality."[111] Nationalism and decadence made a "triumph" out of death and degradation, and "an orgy of blood, of voluptuousness, of death" out of the Great War.[112] The worship of death on the Italian front attracted devotees for reasons both similar to and different from D'Annunzio's. Nationalism and lust for power made Benito Mussolini, too, a worshiper of death. An enlisted man fighting on the upper Isonzo front as a *bersagliere* from September 1915 till March 1917, when he was wounded and discharged, Mussolini had a keen eye for everything related to death: the wounded, the corpses, the cemeteries, the graves, and the effect of death on the living. Almost every entry of his war diary alludes to one or more of these aspects of death.

On the way to the rear in the fall of 1915, Mussolini recognizes a cemetery near Caporetto as the final resting place reserved for the *bersaglieri*. He takes note of the big cross at the center, the names of some of the fallen, and the number of the graves—more than a hundred. Fifteen days later, on the way back to the front, he pays a long visit to the cemetery at Caporetto. He counts the graves—about four hundred now—reads the names of the fallen, and when a cart carrying two coffins arrives, he helps the grave-diggers unload them. Three months later Mussolini again counts the graves in the cemetery at Caporetto. "Now there are seven hundred of them." He reads on the crosses the names of those comrades who belonged to his battalion.[113]

In the trenches, Mussolini's notes on the wounded and the dead thickly dot his diary entries. When in early 1916 shooting started in earnest in his sector, Mussolini records the movements of the wounded: "I see some lightly wounded soldiers running by. Other wounded are carried on stretchers." From his post he eyes the fresh graves of two soldiers and a sergeant mortally wounded by gunfire. Sent to fetch supplies, he catches sight on Mount Rombon of "our dead in graves scattered around," and of seven crosses near a command post. One evening he witnesses the "macabre scene" of exhuming and removing a corpse. An intense shelling shows him another scene of death—"fragments of human limbs," decomposing Austrian corpses—and another "macabre" spectacle, the remains of the dead being hurled about no-man's-land.[114]

Mussolini's notes show neither fear of nor aversion to death; rather, their regularity and vividness suggest an interest in death as a tool of the tyrant. The threat of death alone, Mussolini discovered even before he got into battle, could help the cause of tyranny. Life in the trenches, he wrote after one month there, is such that "one dies without fighting" unless a man musters "very great moral and physical strength."[115] Such an expenditure of energy will keep him from thinking about or striving for a life lived in dignity, peace, and liberty.

For Mussolini the deadly enemy is simply the booster for the Italians' morale: "It is the presence of the enemy, watching and shooting from fifty or a hundred yards that keeps the soldier's morale high." Death, not guns, leads to victory. and death matters more than victory: "A hundred thousand guns will not yield victory, unless the soldiers are capable of moving out of their positions, of going to the assault, and of facing death."[116] Death, whose risk fortifies the soldier, helps the despot to make conquests; death, whose terror nails man to the battlefield, makes the exercise of despotic power easy. And so Mussolini held death up as a virtue.

In this light the meaning of a sentence in the war diary's dedication, a cryptic sentence no doubt added by its author after the other entries were made, becomes clear: "War has evermore and decidedly convinced me of the necessity of war."[117] By sucking man into the orbit of death, war strengthens the despot's rule. The official color adopted by Fascism gave death the key role in the party's ideology and praxis. Black externalized the appeal of death born on the banks of the Isonzo that was to animate Italy under Fascism. The black standard carried by the leaders, the black shirt and black uniform worn by party members and by the elite troops, testified to Mussolini's lunacy—the belief that life is ruled by death.

In the midst of death, however, men free from political or esthetic aberrations felt a surge of vitality and stood up to the triumph of death sung by men like D'Annunzio and Mussolini. Giuseppe Ungaretti, who ranked with Salvatore Quasimodo and Eugenio Montale among the foremost twentieth-century Italian poets, fought as an infantryman on the lower Isonzo front from December 1915 to the beginning of 1918, and after that on the Western Front with the French. The collections of the war poems he composed at the front, *Il porto sepolto*, *Naufragi*, and *Girovago*, include poems that reflect the experience of his first year of fighting on Mount San Michele, the epicenter of the lower Isonzo front.

Ungaretti's poetry springs, in the words of the poet himself, from a knowledge of "the extreme precariousness of man's life in war," and from the impulse "to exorcise death."[118] The very proximity of death at the front inspires the poet with love of life. On Mount San Michele, Ungaretti recalls in "Note," "I was in the presence of death . . . which I learned to know in a new, terrible fashion. . . . In my poetry . . . in *Il porto sepolto* I exalt almost savagely the will to live *[slancio vitale]*, the appetite for life, which was intensified by the proximity of and daily contact with death."[119]

On August 5, 1916, Ungaretti wrote:

Like this stone
Of S. Michele
so cold
so hard
so dried
so refractory
so totally dispirited

Like this stone
is my lament
that is not seen

Death is paid off
by living.[120]

The poem, entitled "I am a Creature," is the lament of a soldier shorn of human qualities, "like this stone." The soldier laments the idea of living as dying: living at the front as an act of death. The last stanza is also a protest against the absurdity of dying from the viewpoint of a "creature," that is, a being whose essence is life.

The brief "Soldiers," made up of a single simile, represents, too, a kind of death in life:

We are as—
in autumn
on the trees—
leaves.[121]

In the suspended state between life and death, the soldiers have traveled half the distance that separates them from their end, yet they still cling to life. In another poem, "Brothers," the poet responds to the frailty of life in the trenches by longing to be one with his comrades in brotherly love, defying death:

> What is your regiment
> brothers?
>
> Word that trembles
> in the night
> Leaf just born
>
> In quivering air
> involuntary rebellion
> of man facing his
> fragility
>
> Brothers.[122]

Even death in its macabre starkness has no power to sever man from life; death, on the contrary, pulls the poet toward life:

> One whole night
> thrust down beside
> a slaughtered
> comrade
> his snarling
> mouth
> turned to the full moon
> the bloating
> of his hands
> entering
> my silence

I have written
letters full of love

Never have I held
so
fast to life.[123]

In one of the most remarkable of all of Ungaretti's poems, "The Rivers," life surges out of death in an emotional and historical sweep. The occasion of the poem was Ungaretti's bathing in the water of the Isonzo one morning in August 1916. In the first two years of the war the fiercest fighting had raged around the upper and lower reaches of this river. The Isonzo was Ungaretti's combat zone, the deadliest on the Italian front. The last seven stanzas of the poem:

I have gone over
the seasons
of my life

These are
my rivers

This is the Serchio
from whose waters have drawn
perhaps two thousand years
of my farming people
my father and my mother

This is the Nile
that saw me
born and growing
burning with unknowing
on its broad plains

This is the Seine
and in its troubled flow
I was remingled and remade

and came to know myself
These are my rivers
counted in the Isonzo

This is my nostalgia
as it appears
in each river
now it is night
now my life seems to me
a corolla
of shadows.[124]

In the last stanza life has become darkness, symbolizing the death surrounding the poet in the combat zone. By looking first at the end and then back to the three stanzas beginning with "This is," the reader can feel the sense of life that flows from "nostalgia," through the short stanza "These are my rivers / counted in the Isonzo," and that then explodes in the first three stanzas. The first stanzas, "the seasons" of the poet's "life," represent three distinct stages. In the first stanza, "This is the Serchio," the poet imagines the Tuscan river on whose banks (Lucca), Ungaretti's ancestry is rooted. The ancestry is imagined, not as a static thing, but as the progress of succeeding generations for two thousand years, ending with the poet's father and mother. The next stanza portrays the Nile, which flows by Alexandria, the city where the poet was born and grew up. Next is the Seine, evoking Paris, where Ungaretti was born to the world of learning and art. The fourth river, the Isonzo, expresses no vitality. It is the river of death, or, as an earlier stanza of the poem reveals, the tool of degradation, which wears out the soldier-poet and makes of him a lifeless thing. Like the "stone" of "I am a Creature":

This morning I stretched out
in an urn of water

and like a relic
rested
The Isonzo as it flowed
polished me
like one of its stones.[125]

In this river of death, why does the poet take stock of the "seasons" of his life, of the vital moments in his earthly journey? Because he wishes both to affirm the vitality of each of the three "moments" that went before, and to defy the precariousness of life in the death zone. In counting "his" rivers, the poet evokes three milestones of his earthly journey—three moments of vitality—and he clings to them. He sings the song of life that defies impending death—the "night" and the "shadows" that "now" hold sway in the combat zone.

No other writer-combatant shows the *slancio vitale*, the "appetite for life" that distinguishes Ungaretti's work. The impulses are so powerful that they monopolize Ungaretti's imagination and banish the ghastliness of death, which finds no place in Ungaretti's poetry. But the ghastliness of death on the battlefield was too visible and too telling to be ignored by other writers and combatants, who seized the occasion to defy death and cling to life. Henri Barbusse, Isaac Rosenberg, Wilfred Owen, and Jean Giono represent death in different ways, but the prose and poetry of all four express the sense of loss for both the dead and the survivors, a loss beyond the destruction of the body. Betrayal and desecration turn the world of death into a kind of heart of darkness that, condemning itself, demands the light of life.

In the central chapter of Henri Barbusse's *Under Fire*, Corporal Bertrand's men wake up in the morning in their dugouts and behold through the mist the corpses of four comrades retrieved from no-man's-land the day before: Lamuse, Barque, Biquet, and Eudore. Barque's face "is dark and polluted by the clammy stains of disordered hair, and his wide and scalded eyes are heavily encrusted with blackened blood." Biquet's corpse "appears to be under the stress of a huge effort. . . . The extreme exertion overflows upon the protruding cheekbones and forehead of his grimacing face, contorts it hideously . . . divides his jaws in a spectral cry, and spreads wide the eyelids from his lightless troubled eyes." Lamuse's corpse is drained of blood; in its "puffed and creased face," the eyes are "gradually sinking in their sockets, one more than the other. There is "a pestilential vapor" hovering about the remains of these beings with whom, Barbusse now realizes, "we lived so intimately and suffered so long." Death's hideous work alienates the dead comrades from the living, destroys the human bond of life that through piety and remembrance makes for one generation to survive in the next. When we glance at those four corpses, Barbusse writes of himself and his surviving comrades, "We say, 'they are dead, all four'; but they are too far disfigured for us to say truly, 'it is *they*.' "[126] The dead are only four "motionless monsters." The spectacle of their death has killed, in the mind and the hearts of the survivors, what they refuse to lose—the humanity that once bonded Lamuse, Barque, Biquet, and Eudore to their comrades.

In one of the best poems of the Great War,[127] "Dead Man's Dump," Isaac Rosenberg wrote:

> The wheels lurched over sprawled dead
> But pained them not, though their bones crunched.
> Their shut mouths made no moan.
> They lie there huddled, friend and foeman,
> Man born of man, and born of woman,
> And shells go crying over them
> From night till night and now.
> . . . .
> Earth! Have they gone into you!

Somewhere they must have gone,
And flung on your hard back
Is their soul's sack
Emptied of God-ancestralled essences.[128]

Death shows three faces: the desecration of the unburied dead, torn by war's unceasing turmoil; the loss of their soul, "emptied of God-ancestralled essences"; and the dead's expulsion from humanity, for they now belong to the filth and waste of the dump, where no living come to revere and to remember the dead.

In Wilfred Owen's "Anthem for Doomed Youth," the soldier's animal-like manner of dying ("these who die as cattle") deprives him of the rite through which the presence of the dead is preserved by the community of the living. This desecration marks the fallen as lesser men, and the "demented choirs of wailing shells" at their death consign them to oblivion:

What passing-bells for these who die as cattle?
—Only the monstrous anger of the guns.
. . . no prayers, no bells;
Nor any voice of mourning save the choirs—
The shrill, demented choirs of wailing shells.[129]

"Protest against the obscenity of dying"[130] is the theme of Jean Giono, the French novelist and soldier who fought at Verdun and at Chemin des Dames and was wounded at Mount Kemmel. The common fate of men and animals in the Great War is the subject of his novel *Le grand troupeau*, translated into English as *To the Slaughterhouse*—a title that more meaningfully expresses the message of the work. Giono likes to set his scenes in the context of nature, and his predilection shows at the beginning of the novel in the lyrical portrayal of the flock of sheep migrating through the dusty Alpine villages. The shepherds have been sent to war and the flock, neglected, is in bad shape. "Human and animal collectivities are conjoined by suffering"[131] and united in death. The "master-sheep," collapsing in the dust like a heap of shorn wool, foretells the impending death of men in war. To Burle, the demise of the ram is a "waste of life," and to Clerestin, like Burle a peasant, it is a waste of "human" life. "What are we going to do," he asks himself, thinking of the war that will take his sons away from the flock. "We are no race of warriors, that's for sure. My young'un pale and sick, my eldest with his tender feet! And he's got some mysterious illness inside which nobody can put their finger on." But they are to march to war, and the inevitable death it brings.[132]

The central chapter of the novel, "There Will Be No Pity," portrays two scenes: the butchery of animals by the army, and the suffering and dying of the soldiers in the field hospital. A critic calls the chapter "telling."[133] Why is it so? Through simple but gory symbolism, the chapter degrades death and dehumanizes the soldier; physical death signals spiritual death. In portraying animals killed by men and men killed by impotence and indifference and dying like animals, Giono uses the same tone. He fills both scenes with stark anatomical details, with gore, and with brutishness. The dying of animals and the dying of men thus merge; what happens in the butchers' village is the same as what happens in the field hospital, and vice versa. The distinction between man's death and an animal's death is lost.

As the reader enters with Giono in what he styles "the butcher's village," he faces a surrealistic world of slaughter and death: "You had to walk over the bundles of brushwood that filled the holes in the road, and red juice sprang up around your shoes. The streams flowed. Packs of dogs . . . followed the winding stench of death in the air. In the shadow of the open barns, large white forms with short arms were crucified against the walls. Thick bodies were slit down the middle like loaves, only the cracks were gaping red. . . . A man passed with a bucket in his hand. He balanced another bucket on his head with his left arm. It was full to the rim with congealed blood and tripes. Another man walked behind him . . . He carried a large chunk of bleeding beef. . . . In the courtyard you could hear the muffled blows of axes striking into skin and hair. The bullock fell. Its hooves scraped the stone slabs. They pumped air into the belly of a sheep. They tapped the swollen body with an iron rod."

The scene is abruptly interrupted and the narrator shifts focus, first, to Regotax's death, whose face has been mangled into "pulverized flesh and white, bristling little bones," and then to Joseph, one of the walking wounded, from whose right arm "a fountain of blood squirted through his fingers." When Joseph reaches the field hospital a scene from a slaughterhouse confronts him. The air reeks of ether, blood, and iodine; dirty bandages ferment in the corners of the room; the medical officer, a major, struggles with a wounded man on the floor. The major, the only officer in charge, cannot cope with the mass of the wounded, from which "an exposed unblinking eye started up at its eyelid, or an arm held up its crushed hand like a grape, or in place of a stomach a puddle grew larger and overflowed." The major is wallowing in blood and he keeps calling for his aide to fetch dirt to absorb the flood of blood, and to "throw out the corpses," to "throw the corpses in the canal." Like an instrument of evil and destruction, the major presides over the desecration of death: "He looked around him at the blood and the men. They might have been in a butcher's shop. In that little cavern in the ground against the canal bank, they had just emptied stretcher-loads of meat."[134]

In another scene of the same chapter of *To the Slaugh-*

terhouse, Giono uses the image of animals preying on the corpses on the battlefield, an image analogous to Isaac Rosenberg's in "Dead Man's Dump"; it suggests the change of the soldier into what T.E. Lawrence would call "vile matter." The scene may have "horrible beauty," as one critic notes,[135] but it is certainly unique in the fiction of the Great War in representing the desecration of death through a kind of second death—the destruction of human remains by beasts:

> "The rats came to sniff them. They jumped from one corpse to another . . . They sniffed the cheek, then they crouched down into a ball and started eating the flesh between the nose and the mouth, next the edge of the lips, and eventually the green apple of the cheeks. Every now and then the rats cleaned their paws in their whiskers. When they came to the eyes, they scratched them out slowly and licked the eyelids. They bit into the eye as though it was a little egg and chewed it gently, slanting their mouths to suck up the juice. Before dawn was over, the crows arrived on their strong, steady wings. . . . The crows pushed at the helmets. Sometimes, when the corpse was lying in a position to defeat the bird's purpose, the crow pulled at the beard until the area of the neck between beard and chest-hair was exposed. The meat was tender there and quite fresh, the red blood still formed into a little ball. The crows started pecking at once, tearing off the skin, then they ate solemnly, calling out now and then to their mates. . . . Mother crows clicked their beaks with worry in the nests of green and blue cloth, the rats pricked up their ears in the holes which were heated by the hair and beards of men. Big balls of fat white worms rolled over."[136]

But the grief, the warning, and the ideals expressed by the fiction and poetry of death did little to spare the Europeans the consequence of the holocaust—a protracted belief in, and practice of, violence. While the Great War was being fought, the politicians heralded it as the war to end war. Instead the Great War planted the seed of yet another holocaust, in which death would reap another generation of Europeans. The Great War chained its generation to death's way—violence. The war, won and lost by massive slaughter, endorsed death's way, and violence haunted that generation in the war's aftermath. The spirit of revenge, arrogance, and egoism—all forms of mute violence—ruled the victors' dealings with the fallen enemy at Versailles. The victors wanted "to twist the enemy's wrist, where he lay bound, and to run pins into his eyes." A deadly wind was blowing anew and it came, on the one side, from "species of men who passed for Englishmen—as mongrels, curs, sloughs, water-rugs, and demi-wolves are all clept by the name of dogs." At the peace table this "species" of men showed that the old spirit of Prussia, beaten out of the field, "had won in the souls of her conqueror's rulers." At Versailles not one word was written "to bring back some memory of the generosity of [England's] sons," to give death a meaning, to ennoble it. Nothing was proposed to rebuild in the name of hundreds of thousands of dead men a Europe free from the hate and greed that had soiled and ravaged the old world, and thus redeem their death. Nothing was said or done to make sure that Prussian brutality would never again raise its head.[137]

The wind that swept all meaning out of death blew also from the Italian side. Italy's unreasonable demands extended to the peace table the violence of the battlefield. At the end of his collection of letters and diaries of fallen Italian soldiers, Adolfo Omodeo concluded that the aftermath of the war "repudiated the common civilization and faith of those who died" because the force used to prevail over the Austro-

German coalition eclipsed the aims and ideals of the war—freedom for the people oppressed by the Central powers. The brutality of the Prussians on the battlefield contaminated those who fought against it, and when the war was over the Italians made their own explosive show of Prussian violence at Versailles.[138]

But from death the war generation drew, too, spiritual strength and a sense of victory over violence and loss. Impelled to deny death's legacy, the war generation did not forget the dead but idealized their life and strength in the face of doom, keeping them alive in its thought and imagination. Roland Dorgelès, the infantryman, aviator, and author of *Les croix de bois (Wooden Crosses)*, remembered the dead for their spiritual energy and vitality: "You were so young, so confident, so strong," he mourned his fallen comrades. "Ah, no! you should not have died. . . . Such a power of life and joy was in you that it was lord over the blackest trials."[139] The futility of death of comrades haunted the French veteran, and fifty years after the guns of the Great War fell silent, he still asked himself: "Why did we fight? Why did we let ourselves get killed?" Dorgelès was unable to answer these questions and reassure the million and a half who died in the war—as well as himself—that sacrifice and death had done some good to the nations that fought the war.[140] But in a way he had already found an answer to the questions when in *Wooden Crosses* he wrote of the soul of his comrades at the front growing "ever strong and stronger" in the face of the "overwhelming crushing toil of fatigue, in the face of Death himself."[141]

The life of the fallen, their spiritual strength, and their defiance of death would live in the imagination of the survivors, in a second life that denied death. The Italian poet Ungaretti refused to let death snatch his comrades, and in the midst of a disintegrating world, the hell of the Carso, he kept them alive in his poetry:

Of these houses
there remain
but a few
remnants of wall

Of so many
who were linked with me
there remains
not even so much

But in my heart
no cross is missing[142]

Paolo Monelli, who had known the simple life of the *alpini*, pulsating with vitality and generosity, wrote of his fallen comrades: "You are not dead today; you are the tired comrades who, having returned from a long day on the line, are now resting; you are still with us."[143] During Siegfried Sassoon's convalescence in England, the poet realized that what his comrades had endured on the Western Front transcended both patriotism and military duty. Sassoon saw in those who daily faced death in the trenches or on the battlefield the workings of a spirit whose strength defied death itself, and served a cause beyond war: "I was rewarded by an intense memory of men whose courage had shown me the power of the human spirit—that spirit which could withstand the utmost assault. Such men had inspired me to be at my best when things were very bad, and that outweighed all the failures. Against the background of the War and its brutal stupidity those men had stood glorified by the thing which sought to destroy them."[144]

Though far from the battlefield, Georges Duhamel too saw simple soldiers challenge death's legacy and refuse to "die as cattle."[145] The protagonists of *Civilisation 1914–1917* and *Vie des martyrs (The New Book of Martyrs)*, wounded and dying men whom Duhamel lived with and tended as a medical officer in field hospitals, withstand pain and death, not because of their patriotism but because of a newly found sense of human dignity. "Come on, come on," private Calmel heartens his comrades in a hospital ward on the Somme as shells fall close to them, "we are men, aren't we?" As Calmel lies on his bed, wounded and dying, his voice, which imminent death makes authoritative, emits "a spiritual force . . . capable of restoring order and self-confidence in the hearts" of the hospitalized.[146]

Duhamel clarifies the meaning of the words and attitude of men like Calmel at the end of *New Book of Martyrs*: "A whole nation, ten whole nations are learning to live in Death's company. Humanity has entered the wild beast's cage, and sits there with the patient courage of the lion-tamer." In the very midst of death the values that will rescue humanity from the wild beast's cage take shape. Because of "your native goodness," Duhamel addresses again his dying soldiers, and because of "your serene confidence in better times to come . . . I can still believe in the moral future of the world. At the very hour when the . . . instinct inclines the world to ferocity, you preserve, on your beds of suffering, a beauty, a purity of outlook which goes far to atone for the monstrous crime. . . . Your simple grandeur of soul redeems humanity from its greatest crime, and raises it from its deep abyss."[147]

But exceptional men like Ungaretti, Sassoon, and Duhamel were too few, and the voice that said no to war and death was too faint to be heard, too weak to dispel the long shadow death had cast over Europe. Only twenty or so years after those men penned their lines, the specter of death beckoned again and Europe reentered the wild beast's cage.

Conclusion

In some primitive societies, it has been said, battle, maiming, and killing come as less of a shock than in more advanced cultures.[1] Primitive man, von Clausewitz noted early in the nineteenth century, is naturally endowed with a "certain strength of body and soul" that makes him indifferent to "exertion and suffering," makes him brave and fit for war and victory.[2] Anthropologists have confirmed von Clausewitz's view, and have recognized that primitive man is callous to human suffering and to "the enormity of the crime of destroying human life."[3] It is this very callousness that helps produce an efficient warrior. It would seem that by 1914 politicians and generals understood that to endure life and to fight in the trenches the soldier needed something that was missing in twentieth-century man: the toughness of the savage. The trenches and the battlefields returned twentieth-century man to a kind of life that had very little to do with civilization. In the trenches and on the battlefields, twentieth-century man fought, died, survived, and changed for the worse.

In another way degradation served as an inducement to war. The Italian elite, charging the common people with real or imaginary decay, sent them to make war and to die in search of punishment and redemption. Contempt for the people and the dream of redemption explain to some extent the life and the work of D'Annunzio, an intellectual who bandied death about as a kind of welcomed suicide.

The Great War, Barbara Tuchman wrote, was a failure, a tragedy, and a delusion.[4] It settled no political differences among the nations that fought it, but engendered the resentment and the hostility that led to another, bloodier conflict; the realization that men could be used and abused with ease sent Europe back to the battlefield. In the Great War generals and politicians alike became convinced that, since the troops could be treated like cattle, war could be easy and inexpensive. And the politicians finally exploited the sinister legacy of World War I—disregard for the value of human life, which grew into Nazism and Fascism.

Those protagonists of the war who, like Lussu, Sassoon, and Remarque, understood that combat destroyed more than bodies, were rightly concerned about war more as a spiritual and moral loss than as a political blunder or a waste of resources. Their views take on an enhanced meaning today, a time in which those who study the nature of warfare regard the abolition of battle as a distinct possibility.[5] Man may refuse to fight, not because he dreads death—after all, mortals' common fate—but because he refuses to accept what death on the battlefield implies: the destruction of his very essence.

Notes

Preface

1. Andrew Rutherford, *The Literature of War. Five Studies in Heroic Virtue* (London, 1978), p. 1.

2. John Keegan, *The Face of Battle* (New York, 1976), p. 336.

The Animal Within

1. Lewis Mumford, *Technics and Civilization* (New York, 1934), pp. 165, 310; J.F.C. Fuller, *War and Western Civilization 1832-1932* (London, 1932), p. 228.

2. Douglas Jerrold, *The Lie about the War* (London, 1930), p. 30.

3. Keegan, *Face of Battle, p. 275.*

4. *War Letters of Fallen Englishmen,* ed. L. Housman (London, 1930), pp. 117, 118.

5. Ibid., pp. 120, 121.

6. T.E. Lawrence, *Seven Pillars of Wisdom, A Triumph* (New York, 1935), p. 511.

7. G.A. Panichas, introduction to *Promise of Greatness, The War of 1914-1918,* ed. G.A. Panichas (New York, 1968), pp. xxvi-xxvii.

8. Eric Maria Remarque, foreword to *All Quiet on the Western Front,* tr. A.W. Wheen (London, 1929), n.p.

9. *German Students' War Letters,* ed. P. Witkop, tr. A. Wedd (New York, 1929), pp. 162-63.

10. Giani Stuparich, *Guerra del '15* (Turin, 1978), p. 144.

11. Ardengo Soffici, *Kobilek,* vol. 3 of *Opere* (Florence, 1960), pp. 155, 195.

12. Gabriel Chevallier, *La peur* (Paris, 1930), p. 237.

13. Carlo Emilio Gadda, *Il castello di Udine (Turin, 1961),* p. 52.

14. Agostino Gemelli, *Il nostro soldato. Saggi di psicologia militare* (Milan, 1917), pp. 4, 27, 37, 104.

15. Ibid., pp. 45, 22.

16. Adolfo Omodeo, *Momenti della vita di guerra. Dai diari e dalle lettere dei caduti 1915-1918* (Turin, 1968), p. 48.

17. Omodeo, *Lettere 1910-1946* (Turin, 1963), p. 121.

18. Carlo Salsa, *Trincee: Confidenze di un fante* (Milan, 1982), pp. 80-81.

19. Giuseppe Antonio Borgese, *Rubè* (Milan, 1928), pp. 88-89.

20. Omodeo, *Momenti*, p. 213.

21. Letter of February 1916 in *Tutta la guerra. Antologia del popolo italiano sul fronte e nel paese*, ed. G. Prezzolini (Milan, 1968), p. 295.

22. Ernest Hemingway, introduction to *Men at War: The Best Stories of All Time*, ed. E. Hemingway (New York, 1942), p. xxiv.

23. *The Liddell Hart Memoirs 1895-1938* (New York, 1965), 1:17.

24. Remarque, *All Quiet on the Western Front*, p. 154.

25. Emilio Lussu, *Un anno sull'altipiano* (Turin, 1964), pp. 112-113.

26. Robert Graves, *Good-bye to All That* (New York, 1957), pp. 67, 69, 72, 73, 82, 131, 169.

27. Rutherford, *Literature of War*, p. 93.

28. Graves, *Good-bye to All That*, pp. 157, 170.

29. Ibid., pp. 171-72.

30. William Shakespeare, *Othello*, act 2, sc. 3, lines 291-294.

31. Graves, *Good-bye to All That*, p. 172.

32. Ibid., pp. 171-72, 223; Katherine Snipes, *Robert Graves* (New York, 1979), p. 4.

33. *Men who March Away: Poems of the First World War*, ed. I.M. Parsons (New York, 1965), p. 171.

34. Keegan, *Face of Battle*, p. 326.

35. Piero Melograni, *Storia politica della Grande Guerra 1915-1918* (Bari, 1969), pp. 245, 247-48.

36. Lussu, *Un anno sull'altipiano*, p. 38.

37. Ibid., p.97.

38. Ibid., pp. 25, 37, 38, 209.

39. Ibid., pp. 45-46.

40. Ibid., pp. 209, 211.

41. Ibid., pp. 73-74.

42. Siegfried Sassoon, "Memoirs of an Infantry Officer," in *The Memoirs of George Sherston* (New York, 1937), p. 148.

43. Ibid., pp. 194-95.

44. Ibid., pp. 195-96.

45. Ibid., pp. 208-09.

46. Ibid., pp. 228-29.

47. Sassoon, "Sherston's Progress," in *Memoirs of George Sherston*, p. 20; Graves, *Good-bye to All That*, p. 233.

48. Sassoon, "The Dream," in *Collected Poems* (New York, 1949), p. 94.

49. Hemingway, introduction to *Men at War*, p. xiv.

50. Bernard Bergonzi, *Heroes' Twilight: A Study of the Literature of the Great War* (New York, 1966), p. 191.

51. Rutherford, *Literature of War*, p. 105.

52. Michael Howard, introduction to *The Middle Parts of Fortune, Somme and Ancre 1916*, by Frederic Manning (London, 1977), p. vii.

53. Manning, *Middle Parts of Fortune*, p. 201.

54. Ibid., pp. 1, 4, 6-7, 11.

55. Ibid., pp. 7-8, 11, 12.

56. Ibid., pp. 39-40, 141.

57. Ibid., pp. 8-11, 212-18.

58. Richard H. Tawney, *The Attack and Other Papers* (New York, 1953), pp. 14-16.

59. Herbert Read, *The Contrary Experience: Autobiographies* (New York, 1973), pp. 99-100, 212-13, 223, 224.

60. Herbert Read, "The Happy Warrior," in *Naked Warriors* (London, 1919), p. 26.

61. "I want to mix a few sacred Apollonian English ashes with theirs [French heroes'] lest England be shamed." *The Letters of Rupert Brooke*, ed. G. Keynes (New York, 1968), p. 655.

62. Robert Wohl, *The Generation of 1914* (Cambridge, Mass., 1979), p. 85; Denis Winter, *Death's Men: Soldiers of the Great War* (London, 1978), p. 32.

63. T.E. Hulme, *Further Speculations*, ed. S. Hynes (Minneapolis, 1955), pp. 200-202.

64. Bertrand Russell, *The Ethics of War: Bertrand Russell and Ralph Barton Perry on World War I* (New York, 1972), p. 61.

65. Ibid., pp. 63, 106-07.

66. Benedetto Croce, *L'Italia dal 1914 al 1918: Pagine sulla guerra* (Bari, 1965), pp. 111-12.

67. Herbert Read, *A Coat of Many Colours* (London, 1956), p. 21.

68. Colin Wilson, *The Outsider* (New York, 1956), p. 73.

69. Ibid., p. 72.

70. John Mack, *A Prince of Our Disorder: The Life of T.E. Lawrence* (Boston, 1976), pp. 456, 457.

71. Arnold W. Lawrence, ed., *T.E. Lawrence by His Friends* (London, 1937), p. 272.

72. Mack, *Prince of Our Disorder*, p. 242.
73. *The Letters of T.E. Lawrence*, ed. D. Garnett (London, 1938), p. 411.
74. Ibid., p. 411; Mack, *Prince of Our Disorder*, p. 342.
75. *Letters of T.E. Lawrence*, pp. 409, 410.
76. Dan. 4:32-33.
77. *Letters of T.E. Lawrence*, pp. 413, 415.
78. Lawrence, *Seven Pillars of Wisdom*, p. 247.
79. Ibid., p. 468.
80. Read, *Coat of Many Colours*, pp. 24-25.
81. Mack, *Prince of Our Disorder*, p. 456.
82. Lawrence, *Seven Pillars of Wisdom*, p. 502.
83. Ibid., pp. 466, 468.
84. Ibid., pp. 29, 30.
85. Ibid., pp. 31-32; Mack, *Prince of Our Disorder*, p. 213.
86. Lawrence, *Seven Pillars of Wisdom*, pp. 562, 564.
87. Ibid., pp. 641, 642.
88. Mack, *A Prince of Our Disorder*, p. 241.
89. Lawrence, *Seven Pillars of Wisdom*, p. 659.
90. Ezra Pound, *Gaudier-Brzeska: A Memoir* (London, 1960), p. 27.
91. Ibid., pp. 20, 21, 70, 73.
92. Benito Mussolini, *Il mio diario di guerra (1915-1917)*, in *Opera omnia*, ed. E.D. Susmel (Florence, 1961), 34:27.
93. Ibid., p. 27.
94. Pierre Teilhard de Chardin, "La nostalgie du front," in *Ecrits du temps de la guerre 1916-1919* (Paris, 1965), pp. 206, 207-08.
95. Ibid., pp. 213-14.
96. The war, wrote the French Jesuit in 1918 from the trenches, has brought down "the whole structure of a decayed civilization." "La grande monade," in *Ecrits*, p. 238.
97. Thomas Mann in 1915, quoted by Fritz Stern, *The Politics of Despair* (Berkeley and Los Angeles, 1961), p. 206, and by Barbara Tuchman, *The Guns of August* (New York, 1962), p. 311.
98. Friedrich von Bernhardi, *Germany and the Next War*, tr. A.H. Fowles (New York, 1914), pp. 11, 17.
99. Ernst Junger, *The Storm of Steel*, tr. B. Creighton (New York, 1975), p. 1.
100. Ibid., p. 7.
101. Ibid., pp. 22, 29, 38, 39.
102. Ibid., pp. 92-93.

103. Ibid., p. 70.

104. Ibid., pp. 254-55, 262-63.

105. Gerhard Loose, *Ernst Junger* (New York, 1974), p. 28.

106. Junger, *Copse 125: A Chronicle from the Trench Warfare of 1918*, tr. B. Creighton (London, 1930), p. 89.

107. Junger, *Storm of Steel*, p. 209.

108. Jules Romains, *Verdun*, tr. G. Hopkins (New York, 1939), pp. 432, 433.

109. Loose, *Ernst Junger*, p. 115.

110. Ibid., p. 21.

111. Friedrich Nietzsche, *On the Genealogy of Morals*, tr. W. Kaufmann and R. Hollingdale (New York, 1969), pp. 40-41, 86.

112. Junger, *Copse 125*, pp. 190, 191.

113. Ernst Junger, *Der Kampf als Inneres Erlebnis*, in *Werke* (Stuttgart, 1960), 5:17-18, 45.

114. Attilio Frescura, *Diario di un imboscato*, in *Tre Romanzi della grande guerra*, ed. M. Schettini (Milan, 1966), pp. 124-25.

115. Ibid., pp. 130-31.

116. Ibid., p. 133.

117. Henri Barbusse, *Under Fire*, tr. W. Wray (London, 1974), pp. 247, 250.

118. Ibid., pp. 252, 253.

119. Ibid., pp. 256, 340-41.

120. Jonathan King, "Henri Barbusse: *Le feu* and the Crisis of Social Realism," in *The First World in Fiction: A Collection of Critical Essays*, ed. H. Klein (London, 1977), p. 51.

121. Barbusse, *Under Fire*, pp. 257, 342.

122. Remarque, *All Quiet on the Western Front*, pp. 18, 20.

123. Ibid., pp. 7, 155. The novel places unusual stress on food and bodily functions. For instance: "The soldier is on friendlier terms than other men with his stomach and intestines. Three quarters of his vocabulary is derived from these regions, and they give an intimate flavour to expressions of his deepest indignation." Ibid., p. 15. On this aspect: C. Barker and R. Last, *Erich Maria Remarque* (London, 1979), pp. 50, 56.

124. Remarque, *All Quiet on the Western Front*, pp. 29-30.

125. Rudolf Binding, *A Fatalist at War*, tr. I. Morrow (Boston, 1929), p. 78.

126. Remarque, *All Quiet on the Western Front*, p. 30.

127. Ibid., pp. 35, 65-66, 154-55.

128. Ibid., p. 112.
129. Ibid., p. 113, 115, 118, 121.
130. Ibid., pp. 126-127, 129, 131-32.
131. Ibid., pp. 135-136, 137, 154.
132. Ibid., pp. 296-97.
133. *German Students' War Letters*, pp. 20-21.

2. A Bath of Black Blood

1. Renato Serra, *Ultime lettere dal campo*, in *Esame di coscienza di un letterato* (Rome, 1973), p. 79.
2. Benedetto Croce, *Storia d'Italia dal 1871 al 1915* (Bari, 1928), p. 293.
3. Adolfo Omodeo, *Momenti della vita di guerra. Dai diari edalle lettere dei caduti 1915-1918* (Turin, 1968), p. 176; Mario Isnenghi, *Il mito della grande guerra da Marinetti a Malaparte* (Bari, 1970), p. 137.
4. Serra, *Esame di coscienza di un letterato*, pp. 39, 43, 44, 45, 48.
5. Ibid., p. 51.
6. Ibid., pp. 47, 49-50.
7. Ibid., pp. 62, 63.
8. Renato Serra, "Partenza di un gruppo di soldati per la Libia," in *Scritti*, ed. G. de Robertis and A. Grilli (Florence, 1958), 2:525.
9. Serra, *Esame di coscienza di un letterato*, p. 64.
10. G. A. Borgese, *Rubè* (Milan, 1928), pp. 29, 30, 31, 32, 34.
11. Ibid., pp. 88-91.
12. Ibid., pp. 419-20.
13. Robert Soucy, *Fascist Intellectual: Drieu La Rochelle* (Berkeley and Los Angeles, 1979), p. 53.
14. Pierre Drieu La Rochelle, *État civil* (Paris, 1949), pp. 23, 24; Soucy, *Fascist Intellectual*, pp. 25, 27, 28, 53.
15. Pierre Drieu La Rochelle, *Sur les écrivains*, ed. F. Grover (Paris, 1964), p. 87; idem, *La comédie de Charleroi* (Paris, 1934), pp. 31, 33; Soucy, *Fascist Intellectual*, pp. 51, 52.
16. Drieu, *La comédie de Charleroi*, pp. 28-29.
17. Drieu, *Sur les écrivains*, p. 36; idem, *La comédie de Charleroi*, pp. 49, 50, 56, 58-59.
18. Drieu, "Le lieutenant de tirailleurs," in *La comédie de Charleroi*, p. 194.

19. Croce, *L'Italia dal 1914 al 1918*, pp. 26-29.

20. Ibid., pp. 221, 224.

21. Omodeo, *Momenti*, pp. 170-71.

22. G.A. Borgese, *Goliath: The March of Fascism* (New York, 1937), pp. 82-83.

23. John A. Thayer, *Italy and the Great War: Politics and Culture 1870-1915*, in *Italy from the Risorgimento to Fascism. An Inquiry into the Origins of the Totalitarian State*, by A. William Salomone (New York, 1970), p. 98. On "questions about national worth" see David Roberts, "Croce and Beyond: Italian Intellectuals and the First World War," in *The International History Review* 3 (1981): 203.

24. Eugenio Garin, *Cronache di filosofia italiana 1900-1943* (Bari, 1966), 2:314.

25. Enrico Corradini, *Per la guerra d'Italia* (Rome, 1915), pp. 37-38.

26. Luigi Russo, *Vita e disciplina militare* (Bari, 1946), pp. 27, 29, 38.

27. Omodeo, *Momenti della vita di guerra*, p. 128.

28. Angelo Romano, introduzione to *La cultura italiana del '900 attraverso le riviste* (Turin, 1960), 3:20; Robert Wohl, *The Generation of 1914* (Cambridge, Mass., 1979), p. 165.

29. Giovanni Boine, *Discorsi militari*, in *Il peccato e le altre opere* (Parma, 1971), pp. 629-30.

30. Hegel, *The Phenomenology of Mind*, tr. J. B. Baillie (London and New York, 1949), pp. 473-74.

31. Russo, *Vita e disciplina militare*, pp. 29-30.

32. Ibid., pp. 11, 12.

33. Boine, *Discorsi militari*, p. 617.

34. Croce, *L'Italia dal 1914 al 1918*, pp. 32, 92-93.

35. Ibid., pp. 291, 294.

36. Ibid., pp. 81-83.

37. Filippo Tommaso Marinetti, *L'alcova d'acciaio* (Milan, 1927), pp. 107-08.

38. Giovanni Papini, "Campagna per il forzato risveglio," *Il leonardo*, vol. 3 of *La cultura italiana del '900 attraverso le riviste*, ed. D. Frigessi (Turin, 1960), pp. 313, 314.

39. Giovanni Papini, *Un uomo finito* (Florence, 1932), pp. 20, 169-171, 195-196, 202.

40. Giovanni Papini and Giuseppe Prezzolini, *Vecchio e nuovo nazionalismo* (Milan, 1914), pp. 13-14.

41. Giuseppe Prezzolini, *Caporetto*, in *Il meglio di Giuseppe Prezzolini* (Milan, 1957), pp. 244, 270.

42. Giuseppe Prezzolini and Ardengo Soffici, *Carteggio*, ed. M. Richter (Rome, 1977), 1:301.

43. Ardengo Soffici, *Errore di coincidenza*, vol. 3 of *Opere* (Florence, 1960), pp. 57-58.

44. Piero Jahier, *Con me e con gli alpini*, vol. 3 of *Opere* (Florence, 1967), pp. 115, 128.

45. Paolo Monelli, *Le scarpe al sole* (Milan, 1966), pp. 39, 52.

46. Jahier, *Con me e con gli alpini*, pp. 222-23.

47. Monelli, *Le scarpe al sole*, pp. 52, 194.

48. Carlo Emilio Gadda, *Il castello di Udine* (Turin, 1961), p. 38.

49. Carlo Emilio Gadda, *Giornale di guerra per l'anno 1916*, in *Giornale di guerra e di prigionia* (Turin, 1965), p. 260.

50. Ibid., pp. 170-71.

51. Ibid., pp. 165-66.

52. Gadda, *Il castello di Udine*, pp. 34, 38.

53. Ibid., pp. 31-32, 33, 52-53.

54. Gadda, *Giornale di guerra*, pp. 253, 276-77. On the emotional environment of war and "sublime feeling" as degradation, see J. Glenn Gray, *The Warriors* (New York, 1970), pp. 28, 33. The translator of the passage from Dante is John Sinclair, *Purgatory* (Oxford, 1977), p. 399.

55. Hans Kohn, "The Crisis in European Thought and Culture," in *World War I: A Turning Point in Modern History*, ed. J. Roth (New York, 1967), p. 33.

56. Filippo Marinetti, *Guerra sola igiene del mondo* (Milan, 1915), p. 147.

57. Ibid., p. 148.

58. Giovanni Papini, "Amiamo la guerra!" *Lacerba*, vol. 4 of *La cultura italiana del '900 attraverso le riviste*, ed. G. Scalia (Turin, 1961), p. 329.

59. Giovanni Papini, "La vita non è sacra," *Lacerba*, vol. 4 of *La cultura italiana del '900 attraverso le riviste*, p. 208.

60. Ibid., p. 207.

61. Giovanni Papini, "Dichiarazione d'amore," in *Tutta la guerra*, ed. G. Prezzolini (Milan, 1968), p. 361.

62. Borgese, *Goliath: The March of Fascism*, pp. 111-112.

63. Alberto Monticone, *Gli italiani in uniforme 1915-1918: Intellettuali, borghesi e disertori* (Bari, 1972), p. 85.

64. Olindo Malagodi, *Conversazioni della guerra 1914-1919*, ed. B. Vigezzi (Milan-Naples, 1960), 1:56, 61.

65. Piero Melograni, *Storia politica della Grande Guerra 1915-1918* (Bari, 1969), p. 1; Denis Mack Smith, *Italy: A Modern History* (Ann Arbor, 1969), p. 300.

66. In relating these events I rely on the work of an ex-prime minister, Ivanoe Bonomi, *La politica italiana da Porta Pia a Vittorio Veneto 1870-1918* (Turin, 1944), pp. 273-77.

67. This is Franceso Nitti's view, as reported by Mack Smith, *Italy*, p. 303. Nitti was Italy's prime minister from 1919 to 1920.

68. Robert Wohl, *The Generation of 1914*, p. 170.

69. Piero Pieri, *L'italia nella prima guerra mondiale* (Turin, 1968), p. 74; Smith, *Italy*, p. 304; Paolo Rossi, *Storia d'Italia dal 1815 al 1914* (Milan, 1972), 3:330.

70. Gabriele D'Annunzio, *Per la più grande Italia*, in *Prose di ricerca, di lotta, di comando* (Milan, 1958), 1:59, 62.

71. Bonomi, *La politica italiana*, p. 276.

72. Benito Mussolini, *Opera omnia*, ed. E. and D. Susmel (Florence, 1962), 7:6-7.

73. Ibid., p. 82.

74. Ibid., p. 197.

75. Roland Stromberg, *Redemption by War: The Intellectuals and 1914* (Lawrence, 1982).

76. Croce, *L'Italia dal 1914 al 1918*, p. 291.

77. Pieri, *L'Italia nella prima guerra mondiale*, p. 62.

78. Omodeo, *Momenti*, p. 163.

79. Angelo Gatti, *Caporetto: Dal diario di guerra inedito (maggio-dicembre 1917)*, ed. A. Monticone (Bologna, 1964), pp. 414, 421-22.

80. Lord Moran, *The Anatomy of Courage* (London, 1945), p. 170.

81. Keegan, *Face of Battle*, p. 256.

82. C.E. Montague, *Disenchantment* (London, 1924), p. 3.

83. Housman, *War Letters*, p. 210.

84. Winston Churchill, *The World Crisis* (New York, 1931), p. 568.

85. Henri Massis, "The War We Fought," in *Promise of Greatness: The War of 1914-1918*, ed. G.A. Panichas (New York, 1968), p. 275. Italics are mine.

86. Wohl, *Generation of 1914*, p. 12.

87. Quoted by Henri Massis, *Les jeunes gens d'aujourd'hui* (Paris, 1913), pp. 188, 190.
88. *Memoirs du Marechal Joffre 1910-1917* (Paris, 1932), 1:31.
89. Henri Bergson, *La signification de la guerre* (Paris, n.d.), p. 22. Written in 1915.
90. Tuchman, *Guns of August*, p. 83.
91. Melograni, *Storia politica della Grande Guerra*, pp. 34, 35.
92. Pieri, *L'Italia nella prima guerra mondiale*, p. 87.
93. Melograni, *Storia politica della Grande Guerra*, p. 44.
94. Enrico Caviglia, *Diario* (Rome, 1952), p. 116.
95. Basil Liddell Hart, *Through the Fog of War* (London, 1938), p. 26.
96. Melograni, *Storia politica della Grande Guerra*, pp. 43.
97. Liddell Hart, *A History of the World War 1914-1918* (Boston, 1935), p. 397.
98. Churchill, *The World Crisis*, p. 575.
99. Robert Blake, ed., *The Private Papers of Douglas Haig 1914-1919* (London, 1952), pp. 46-47; Liddell Hart, *A History of the World War*, p. 494.
100. Cyril Falls, *The Great War* (New York, 1959), p. 236.
101. Gatti, *Caporetto*, p. 152.
102. Ibid., p. 147.
103. Ibid., pp. 63-64.
104. Ibid., p. 146.
105. Luigi Gasparotto, *Diario di un deputato* (Milan, 1945), p. 105.
106. Melograni, *Storia politica della Grande Guerra*, pp. 217-219.
107. Gatti, *Caporetto*, pp. 106-07.
108. Malagodi, *Conversazioni della guerra*, 1:106.
109. Cesare de Simone, *Soldati e generali a Caporetto* (Rome, 1970), p. 200.
110. Luigi Cadorna, *La guerra alla fronte italiana* (Milan, 1921), 1:34.
111. Ibid., 1:32-33, 57, 58.
112. Ibid., 1:28, 29, 30.
113. Ibid., 1:28.
114. Gatti, *Caporetto*, p. 285.
115. Malagodi, *Conversazioni della guerra*, 1:210.
116. Ugo Ojetti, *Lettere alla moglie 1915-1919* (Florence, 1964), p. 441.

117. Cadorna, *La guerra*, 1:28, 59.

118. These events found imaginative representation in Ernest Hemingway, *A Farewell to Arms* (New York, 1957), pp. 222-33.

119. Mario Silvestri, *Isonzo 1917* (Turin, 1965), p. 107; Gatti, *Caporetto*, p. 32.

120. Luigi Capello, *Caporetto: Perche?* (Turin, 1967), p. 7.

121. Idem, *Note di guerra* (Milan, 1920), 1:xiii-xiv.

122. Ibid., 2:147.

123. Ibid., 1:105.

124. Ibid., 1:113.

125. Melograni, *Storia politica della Grande Guerra*, pp. 31-32.

126. Capello, *Note di guerra*, 1:318.

127. Ibid., 1:318-19.

128. Mussolini, *Il mio diario di guerra (1915-1917)*, vol. 34 of *Opera omnia*, p. 69.

129. Capello, *Note di guerra*, 1:318-19.

130. Lussu, *Un anno sull'altipiano*, p. 105.

131. Ibid., pp. 105-07.

132. Ibid., pp. 104, 110.

133. Ibid., p. 182.

134. Gatti, *Caporetto*, p. 97.

135. Ibid., p. 98; Carlo Salsa, *Trincee*, p. 62.

136. Monelli, *Le scarpe al sole*, p. 119.

137. Malagodi, *Conversazioni della guerra*, 1:77. This information, given by General Cadorna, may be inaccurate.

138. Salsa, *Trincee*, pp. 60-61.

139. Ibid., p. 61-62.

140. Ibid., p. 63.

141. Luigi Albertini, *Venti anni di vita politica* (Bologna, 1952), 2:106.

142. Ibid., 3:164.

143. Pieri, *L'Italia nella prima guerra mondiale*, pp. 204-05.

144. Lussu, *Un anno sull'altipiano*, pp. 94, 111.

145. Ibid., pp. 178-82.

3. A Loss beyond Life

1. Croce, *L'Italia dal 1914 al 1918*, pp. 145-46.

2. Adolfo Omodeo, *Lettere 1910-1946* (Turin, 1963), pp. xxxvii, 278.

3. Giani Stuparich, *Guerra del '15* (Turin, 1961), pp. 45, 78-79.

4. *Wilfred Owen: Collected Letters*, ed. H. Owen and J. Bell (London, 1967), pp. 449-50.

5. Salsa, *Trincee*, p. 33.

6. Lussu, *Un anno sull'altipiano*, pp. 16-17.

7. Attilio Frescura, *Diario di un imboscato*, p. 68.

8. Siegfried Sassoon, "The General," in *Collected Poems* (New York, 1949), p. 75.

9. Cf. Jon Silkin's interpretation of "The General" in his *Out of Battle: The Poetry of the Great War* (London, 1972), p. 160.

10. Graves, *Good-bye to All That*, p. 149; Alan Clark, *The Donkeys* (New York, 1965), p. 168.

11. Louis-Ferdinand Céline, *Journey to the End of the Night*, tr. J. Marks (Boston, 1934), pp. 50, 55-56, 61-62. On Céline and death: Maurice Rieuneau, *Guerre et révolution dans le roman francais de 1919 a 1939* (Paris, 1974), p. 306.

12. J.F.C. Fuller, *War and Civilization 1832-1932* (London, 1932), p. 227.

13. Ibid., p. 226.

14. Liddell Hart, *Through the Fog of War*, p. 25.

15. Clark, *The Donkeys*, pp. 125, 134, 154, 156.

16. Liddell Hart, *Through the Fog of War*, p. 30.

17. Keegan, *Face of Battle*, pp. 255-56.

18. Graves, *Good-bye to All That*, pp. 162-63.

19. Adrien Bertrand, *L'appel du sol* (Paris, 1916), pp. 84-85.

20. Clark, *The Donkeys*, pp. 156-57.

21. Curzio Malaparte, *Viva Caporetto*! (Milan, 1981), pp. 69, 70-71.

22. Paolo Monelli, *Le scarpe al sole* (Milan, 1966), pp. 123-24.

23. Gatti, *Caporetto*, pp. 61, 91.

24. Stuparich, *Guerra del '15*, p. 56.

25. Lussu, *Un anno sull'altipiano*, pp. 53-54.

26. Ibid., pp. 21, 79-83.

27. Lord Moran, *The Anatomy of Courage* (London, 1945), p. 157.

28. Graves, *Good-bye to All That*, pp. 170-71.

29. Sassoon, "Memoirs of an Infantry Officer," in *The Memoirs of George Sherston* (New York, 1967), p. 284.

30. Sassoon, "To Any Dead Officer," in *Collected Poems*, p. 84.

31. Omodeo, *Momenti*, p. 77.

32. Ibid., p. 229.

33. Ibid., p. 187.

34. Stuparich, *Guerra del '15*, p. 65.

35. Salsa, *Trincee*, pp. 80-81.

36. Remarque, *All Quiet on the Western Front*, pp. 294, 295.

37. Gabriel Chevallier, *La peur* (Paris, 1930), pp. 203, 205.

38. Rieuneau, *Guerre et révolution*, p. 203.

39. Sassoon, "Memoirs of a Fox-Hunting Man," in *The Memoirs of George Sherston*, pp. 372-73. Cf. the strange interpretation of this passage in Eric Leed, *No Man's Land. Combat and Identity in World War I*, (Cambridge, 1979), p. 22: Sassoon wants death because "his home had been so radically transformed by war that there no longer seemed anything secure to which he might return."

40. Bernard Bergonzi, *Heroes' Twilight: A Study of The Literature of the Great War* (New York, 1965), p. 70.

41. Edmund Blunden, *Undertones of War* (New York, 1929), p. 139.

42. Ibid., p. 14; cf. Robert Graves, "The Kaiser's War: A British Point of View," in *Promises of Greatness*, ed. G. Panichas, p. 10. On this aspect: Paul Fussell, *The Great War and Modern Memory* (New York, 1975), pp. 71-74.

43. H.W. Baldwin, *World War I* (New York, 1962), p. 53.

44. Jules Romains, *Verdun*, tr. G. Hopkins (New York, 1939), p. 73.

45. Manning, *The Middle Parts of Fortune*, pp. 146, 147, 154.

46. Sassoon, "To Any Dead Officer," in *Collected Poems*, p. 85.

47. Gatti, *Caporetto*, p. 208.

48. Piero Melograni, *Storia politica della Grande Guerra 1915-1918* (Bari, 1969), p. 292.

49. Gatti, *Caporetto*, pp. 208, 209.

50. J. Glenn Gray, *The Warriors. Reflections on Men in Battle* (New York, 1959), p. 101.

[51]Remarque, *All Quiet on the Western Front*, p. 148; cf. Roland Dorgelès, *Wooden Crosses* (London, 1920), p. 291: coming out of an action alive is the combatant's real "victory" in war. (No translator's name is given for the French novel.)

52. Dominic Hibberd ed., *Poetry of the First World War: A Casebook* (London, 1981), p. 83.

53. Wilfred Owen, "The Next War," in *War Poems and Others*, ed. D. Hibberd (London, 1973), pp. 75-76.

54. Henri Barbusse, *Under Fire*, tr. W.F. Wray (London, 1974), p. 265.

55. Lawrence, *Seven Pillars of Wisdom*, p. 308.

56. Ibid., pp. 30, 307.

57. Lussu, *Un anno sull'altipiano*, pp. 94-95.

58. Gemelli, *Il nostro soldato*, p. 56.

59. Richard Aldington, "Barrage," in *Poems of the War and the Peace*, ed. S. Leonard (New York, 1921), p. 61.

60. Gemelli, *Il nostro soldato*, p. 56.

61. Junger, *Storm of Steel*, pp. 178-79, 314-15.

62. Quoted by Melograni, *Storia politica della Grande Guerra*, pp. 99-100.

63. Stuparich, *Guerra del '15*, p. 130.

64. *German Students' War Letters*, p. 151.

65. Ghisalberti quoted in Melograni, *Storia politica della Grande Guerra*, p. 99.

66. Attilo Frescura, *Diario di un imboscato*, in *Tre romanzi*, pp. 101-102.

67. Jean Bernier, *La percée* (Paris, 1920), p. 256.

68. Richard Aldington, *Death of a Hero* (New York, 1929), pp. 302, 386, 391, 392.

69. Bergonzi, *Heroes' Twilight*, p. 183.

70. Fuller, *War and Civilization*, pp. 226-27.

71. Remarque, *All Quiet on the Western Front*, p. 320.

72. Ibid., pp. 20-30, 35-42.

73. Ibid., pp. 37, 38, 40.

74. Ibid., pp. 287-88, 318.

75. J.S. Untermeyer, "During Darkness," in *Poems of the War and the Peace*, p. 112.

76. Sassoon, "I Stood with the Dead," in *Collected Poems*, p. 103.

77. Sassoon, "Memoirs of an Infantry Officer," in *The Memoirs of George Sherston*, pp. 88-90.

78. Manning, *The Middle Parts of Fortune*, pp. 217-18.

79. Owen, "Apologia pro Poemate Meo," in *War Poems and Others*, p. 82.

80. Lawrence, *Seven Pillars of Wisdom*, pp. 632-33.

81. Mack, *Prince of Our Disorder*, p. 242.

82. "War produced comradeship, which produced vengeance, which in turn, produced war." Tony Ashworth, *Trench Warfare 1914-1918: The Live and Let Live System* (New York, 1980), p. 208.

83. Lussu, *Un anno sull'altipiano*, pp. 133-38.

84. B.L. Knapp, *Georges Duhamel* (New York, 1972), p. 46.

85. Georges Duhamel, *The New Book of Martyrs*, tr. F. Simmonds (London, 1918), pp. 210-11.

86. Romains, *Verdun*, pp. 151–54.

87. On Romains and Freud: Denis Boak, *Jules Romains* (New York, 1974), p. 93.

88. Sigmund Freud, *Reflections on War and Death*, tr. A. Brill and A. Kuttner (New York, 1918), pp. 47, 50-51, 60-61, 70.

89. Giovanni Papini, "Amiamo la guerra!" *Lacerba*, vol. 4 of *La cultura italiana del '900 attraverso le riviste*, ed. G. Scalia (Turin, 1961) p. 330.

90. Giuseppe de Robertis, "Consigli del librario," *La voce (1914-1916)*, vol. 4 of *La cultura italiana del '900 attraverso le riviste*, ed. G. Scalia (Turin, 1961) p. 552.

91. Giuseppe Prezzolini, *Tutta la guerra: Antologia del popolo italiano sul fronte e nel paese* (Milan, 1968), p. 19.

92. Riccardo Bacchelli, *Memorie del tempo presente* (Milan, 1953), p. 105.

93. Corrado Alvaro, *Vent'anni* (Milan, 1953), pp. 133-35.

94. Soffici, *Kobilek*, p. 122.

95. Gabriele D'Annunzio, *Le tre redazioni di un taccuino di guerra*, ed. A. Bruers (Milan, 1942), pp. 20, 22.

96. Gabriele D'Annunzio, *The Triumph of Death*, tr. G. Harding (New York, 1975), pp. 65-66.

97. Gabriele D'Annunzio, *Notturno*, vol. 1 of *Prose di ricerca, di lotta, di comando* (Milan, 1958), pp. 187, 198, 203, 209, 212-13.

98. Ibid., 1:359.

99. Ibid., 1:359-60.

100. Guillaume Apollinaire, "The Hills," in *Calligrammes: Poems of Peace and War (1913-1916)*, tr. A.H. Greet (Los Angeles, 1980), p. 39.

101. Wyndham Lewis, *Blasting and Bombardiering* (London, 1937), pp. 120-122.

102. Tommaso Marinetti, *Uccidiamo il chiaro di luna*! (Milan, 1911), pp. 4-5, 7.

103. Papini, "Amiamo la guerra!" *Lacerba*, in *La cultura italiana del '900*, 4:331.

104. D'Annunzio, *Notturno*, 1:307-08.

105. Junger, *Copse 125*, p. 91.

106. Pierre Drieu La Rochelle, *La comédie de Charleroi*, pp. 49, 59-60.

107. D'Annunzio, *Notturno*, 1:326-327.

108. D'Annunzio, *Il libro ascetico della giovane Italia*, in *Prose di ricerca*, 1:522.

109. Ibid., I, 781-82.

110. Ibid., I, 775, 782.

111. G.A. Borgese, *Gabriele D'Annunzio (Da Primo Vere a Fedra)* (Milan, 1932), p. 205. On "barbarism" and "lack of humanity" in D'Annunzio's writings, see Mario Praz, *The Romantic Agony*, tr. A. Davidson (New York, 1960), p. 387.

112. Gaetano Salvemini, *La politica estera italiana dal 1871 al 1915*, in *Opere*, ed. A. Torre (Milan, 1970), vol. 3, pt. 4, 504.

113. Mussolini, *Diario di guerra*, vol. 34 of *Opera omnia*, pp.46-48, 50.

114. Ibid., pp. 52, 53, 55, 57, 84, 107, 108.

115. Ibid., pp. 28.

116. Ibid., pp. 34, 42, 69.

117. Ibid., pp. 3.

118. Giuseppe Ungaretti, "Note," in *Vita d'un uomo: Tutte le oepre*, ed. L. Piccioni (Milan, 1970), pp. 517, 521.

119. Ibid., p. 521.

120. *Selected Poems of Giuseppe Ungaretti*, tr. A. Mandelbaum (Ithaca, 1975), p. 23.

121. Ibid., p. 55.

122. Ibid., p. 19.

123. Ibid., p. 13.

124. Ibid., p. 27.

125. Ibid., p. 25.

126. Barbusse, *Under Fire*, pp. 227-28.

127. Fussell, *The Great War and Modern Memory*, p. 250.

128. Isaac Rosenberg, "Dead Man's Dump," in *Collected Poems*, ed. G. Bottomly and D. Harding (London, 1949), p. 81. A poem such as this makes it impossible to accept Sir Maurice Bowra's view that the soldier "in constant contact with death . . . usually observed a private fatalism," for he "knew that it was useless to lament or to do anything but hide his feelings": Bowra, *Poetry and the First World War* (Oxford, 1961), p. 20.

129. Owen, "Anthem for Doomed Youth," in *War Poems*, p. 76.

130. W.D. Redfern, "Against Nature: Jean Giono and *Le Grande*

Troupeau," in *The First World War in Fiction: A Collection of Critical Essays,* ed. H. Klein (Bristol, 1976), p. 75.

131. Ibid., pp. 73-74.

132. Jean Giono, *To the Slaughterhouse,* tr. N. Glass (London, 1969), p. 14.

133. Redfern, "Against Nature," p. 79.

134. Giono, *To the Slaughterhouse,* pp. 101-02, 105-07.

135. Redfern, "Against Nature," p. 75.

136. Giono, *To the Slaughterhouse,* pp. 91-92.

137. C.E. Montague, *Disenchantment,* pp. 187, 188.

138. Omodeo, *Momenti,* p. 259.

139. Dorgelès, *Wooden Crosses,* p. 294.

140. Roland Dorgelès, "After Fifty Years," in *Promise of Greatness,* ed. G.A. Panichas (New York, 1968), pp. 15-16.

141. Dorgelès, *Wooden Crosses,* p. 294.

142. Ungaretti, "San Martino del Carso," translated by F.J. Jones in his *Giuseppe Ungaretti Poet and Critic* (Edinburg, 1977), pp. 77-78.

143. Monelli, *Le scarpe al sole,* p. 33.

144. Sassoon, "Memoirs of an Infantry Officer," in *Memoirs of George Sherston,* p. 251.

145. John Cruickshank, *Variations on Catastrophe: Some French Responses to the Great War* (Oxford, 1982), p. 87.

146. Georges Duhamel, *Civilisation 1914-1917* (Paris, 1946), p. 45.

147. Duhamel, *The New Book of Martyrs,* p. 213.

Conclusion

1. Keegan, *Face of Battle,* p. 317.

2. Carl von Clausewitz, *On War,* ed. and tr. M. Howard and P. Paret (Princeton, 1976), p. 101.

3. Maurice Davis, *The Evolution of War: A Study of its Role in Early Societies* (Port Washington, N.Y., 1968), p. 55.

4. Tuchman, *Guns of August* p. 441.

5. Keegan, *Face of Battle,* p. 336.

Index

Albertini, Luigi, 92
Aldington, Richard, 116-17
All Quiet on the Western Front (Remarque), 6, 43-48, 106-07, 118-19
Alvaro, Corrado, 125-26
Apollinaire, Guillaume, 129-30

Bacchelli, Riccardo, 125
Barbusse, Henri, 41-42, 112, 140-41
Bergson, Henri, 78
Bernhardi, Friedrich von, 35
Bernier, Jean, 116
Bertrand, Adrien, 101
Binding, Rudolf, 44
Blumenfeld, Franz, 48-49
Blunden, Edmund, 108
Boine, Giovanni, 60-61
Borgese, Giuseppe, 5, 52-53, 71-72; on D'Annunzio, 133
Bowra, Maurice, 167 n. 128
Brooke, Rupert, 22

Cadorna, Luiga, 79-80, 81-84, 92
Campodonico, Angelo, 4
Capello, Luigi, 84-86, 92
Caporetto: dal diario di guerra inedito (Gatti), 76, 80-81, 89-90, 102-03, 110-11
Caporetto: perchè? (Capello), 85
Castello di Udine, Il, 3, 66
Caviglia, Enrico, 79
Céline, Louis Ferdinand, 98-99
Chevallier, Gabriel, 3, 107
Cigliana, Giorgio, 82
Civilisation 1914-1917, 148-49
Clausewitz, Carl von, 150
Comédie de Charleroi, La (Drieu La Rochelle), 54-55, 131
Conversazioni della guerra (Malagodi), 73, 82, 83-84, 90
Corradini, Enrico, 59
Croce, Benedetto, 23-24, 56-57, 61-62, 76, 95

D'Annunzio, Gabriele, 74-75, 126, 127-29, 130, 131-33
Davis, Maurice, 150
"Dead Man's Dump," (Rosenberg), 141-42
Death of a Hero (Aldington), 116-17
De Robertis, Giuseppe, 125
De Vita, Giovanni, 5
Diario di guerra, Il mio (Mussolini), 34, 87, 133-35
Diario di un imboscato (Frescura), 38-41, 97
Discorsi militari (Boine), 60-61

Dorgelès, Roland, 147
Drieu La Rochelle, Pierre, 54-55, 131
Duhamel, George, 122, 148-49

Esame di coscienza di un letterato (Serra), 50-52
Ethics of War, The (Russell), 22-23

Foch, Ferdinand, 77, 80
French, John, 100
Frescura, Attilio, 38-41, 97
Freud, Sigmund, 123-24
Fuller, J.F.C., 99, 117

Gadda, Carlo Emilio, 3, 66-69
Garin, Eugenio, 59
Garrone, Pinotto, 106
Gasparotto, Luigi, 81
Gatti, Angelo, 76, 80-81, 89-90, 102-03, 110-11
Gaudier-Brzeska, Henri, 33
Gemelli, Agostino, 3-4, 113
Ghisalberti, Alberto, 114-16
Giolitti, Giovanni, 73
Giono, Jean, 142-45
Giornale di guerra e prigionia (Gadda), 66-69
Goliath (Borgese), 71-72
Good-bye to All That (Graves), 7-9, 101, 105
Grandmaison, Louis de, 77
Graves, Robert, 7-9, 101, 105
Grenfell, Julian, 2
Guerra del '15 (Stuparich), 3, 6, 96, 103, 106, 115
Guerra sola igiene del mondo (Marinetti), 69-70
Guerra sulla fronte italiana (Cadorna), 82-83, 84

Haig, Douglas, 80
Hemingway, Ernest, 6, 84, 162 n. 118
Hulme, T.E., 22

Italia dal 1914 al 1918, L' (Croce), 23-24, 56-57, 61-62

Jahier, Piero, 65
Jerrold, Douglas, 1
Joffre, Joseph, 78, 80
Journey to the End of Night (Céline), 98-99
Junger, Ernst, 35-37, 114

Lawrence, T.E., 2, 25-30, 31-32, 112-13, 121
Lewis, Wyndham, 130
Libro ascetico della giovane Italia, Il (D'Annunzio), 132-33
Liddell Hart, Basil, 6, 79
Lloyd George, David, 80
Lord Moran, 77, 104
Lussu, Emilio, 6-7, 10,13, 88-89, 93-94, 103-04, 113, 121-22

Malagodi Olindo, 73, 82, 83-84, 90
Malaparte, Curzio, 102
Mann, Thomas, 35
Manning, Frederic, 16-19, 120
Marconi, Paolo, 57-58
Marinetti Filippo, 62, 69-70, 130
Massis, Henri, 78

Memoirs of an Infantry Officer (Sassoon), 13-15, 105, 107, 119-20, 148
Middle Parts of Fortune, The (Manning), 16-19, 120
Momenti della vita di guerra (Omodeo), 4, 5-6, 50, 57-58, 59-60, 95-96, 105-06, 146-47
Monelli, Paolo, 65, 90, 102, 148
Mumford, Lewis, 1
Mussolini, Benito, 34, 75, 87, 133-35

New Book of Martyrs, The (Duhamel), 122, 148-49
Nivelle, Robert, 80
Nostro soldato, Il (Gemelli), 3-4, 113
Note di guerra (Capello), 84-86
Notturno (D'Annunzio), 127-29, 130, 131-32

Ojetti, Ugo, 80, 84
Omodeo, Adolfo, 4, 95-96, 146-47
Owen, Wilfred, 96, 111-12, 120, 142,

Panichas, G.A., 2
Papini, Giovanni, 62-63, 70, 71, 125
Percée, La (Bernier), 116
Peur, La (Chevallier), 3, 107
Pieri, Piero, 93
Popolo d'Italia, Il, 75
Prezzolini, Giuseppe, 63-64, 125
Psichari, Ernest, 78

Read, Herbert, 21, 27-28
Reflections on War and Death (Freud), 123-24
Remarque, Erich Maria, 6, 43-48, 106-07, 118-19
"Rivers, The" (Ungaretti), 138-140
Rohden, Gotthold von, 3
Romains, Jules, 109-10, 122-23
Rosenberg, Isaac, 141-42
Rubè (Borgese), 5, 52-53
Russell, Bertrand, 22-23
Russo, Luigi, 59-61

Salandra, Antonio, 73-74, 76
Salsa, Carlo, 5, 90-92, 97, 106
Salvemini, Gaetano, 133
Sassoon, Siegfried, 13-15, 97-98, 105, 107, 119-20, 148
Scarpe al sole, Le (Monelli), 65, 90, 102, 148
Serra, Renato, 50-52
Seven Pillars of Wisdom (Lawrence), 2, 25-30, 31-32, 112-13, 121
Shakespeare, William, 9
Soffici, Ardengo, 3, 64, 126
Storm of Steel, The (Junger), 35-37, 114
Stromberg, Roland, 75
Stuparich, Giani, 3, 6, 96, 103, 106, 115

Tawney, Richard, 20
Teilhard de Chardin, Pierre, 34
Thomas, Dylan, 111
To the Slaughterhouse (Giono), 142-45
Trabia, Ignazio di, 59-60

Trincee (Salsa), 5, 90-92, 97, 100
Tuchman, Barbara, 79, 150

Uccidiamo il chiaro di luna! (Marinetti), 130
Un anno sull'altipiano (Lussu), 10-13, 88-89, 93-94, 103-04, 113, 121-22
Under Fire (Barbusse), 41-42, 112, 140-41
Undertones of War (Blunden), 108
Ungaretti, Giuseppe, 135-40, 147-48
Uomo finito, Un (Papini), 63

Vent'anni (Alvaro), 125-26
Verdun (Romains), 109-10, 122-23
Vietnam, 4
Vita e disciplina militare (Russo), 59-61
Voce, La, 60, 63, 125

Wohl, Robert, 74